REAL FUN

In REAL ESTATE

INVESTING

And LANDLORDING

By

Alexander B. Brancic, PhD

Edited by
Linda L. and Deborah A. Brancic

Real Fun in Real Estate Investing and Landlording

Published by
Alexander Publishing
1303 Amostown Road, West Springfield, MA 01089
Phone: (413) 732-4808
e-mail: AlexBrancic@Comcast.net
This book is available at quantity discounts for bulk purchases.

International Standard Book Number: ISBN 0-9742517-0-4

Library of Congress Catalog Card Number: (applied for)

Printed in the United States of America
First Printing: July 2003

I would like to thank my wife Linda for the encouragement and support she gave me during the writing of this book.

I also want to thank both my wife Linda and my daughter Deborah for editing the final copy of this book.

Many thanks to my local landlord association board for providing me with some ideas and forms.

To Shannon,

Alex Brančić

TABLE of CONTENTS

Introductory Remarks

This book is based on the actual experience of the author with purchasing and managing investment properties. It is intended to be of invaluable use to any potential real estate entrepreneur and property manager. The book shows techniques for acquiring investment properties, managing them and dealing with sellers, real estate brokers, bankers, contractors and tenants.

A number of anecdotal stories are presented giving a very real picture of how the dealings between different parties happen on a day-to-day basis. Although all the stories are based on facts and real events, the names and places have been changed to protect the identity of participants and places where it happened. Most of the stories presented are given humorous dialogues and twists that the reader can enjoy while learning at the same time. The book gives useful guidelines, forms and notices that could be used by real estate entrepreneurs and property managers with minor modifications, depending on the state one lives in.

A story is presented based on facts about how the author dealt with the bank, which was threatening to foreclose, giving a detailed description of the entire plan and all the events that happened. The plan that the author applied produced success. The bank wrote the debt off and released the borrower from the responsibility to repay. To protect the participants again, the people, places and events are changed and the name of the bank was not disclosed. Any resemblance with real people, places and events is purely coincidental.

Alexander B. Brancic
June 18, 2003

CHAPTER 1

Reasons to get into Real Estate and What this Book is about

Questions that this chapter will try to answer are:

1. What is a Landlord?

2. Why would a person want to buy properties and become a Landlord?

3. What is this book about and how is it different from the other "Get Rich in Real Estate" kinds of books?

Landlord and Landlording

There are some common myths and misconceptions in the general population about property owners. Here are some of them given through examples and experience.

An average person who is renting an apartment and working for a living has the following impression of a Landlord:

- Landlord is a person who comes monthly to collect a rent check from me. He comes with a receipt book and leaves with a wallet full of money.

- This person does not have to work! He just collects rents and goes on vacations. What an easy way of living that is!

Real Estate professionals, brokers or sellers give very common advice to all young couples: "The best thing for one to do is to buy a 2 Family or a 3-Family house, move into one apartment and have the other tenant pay for most or all of mortgage expenses, so you end up living for free. In addition, after the 20 to 30 years of mortgage payments, tenants have paid off your house and you are still making money on renting the other apartment(s)."

The above advice holds only partial truth. Renting one apartment of the 2-family house may be a good financial strategy, but this puts you in the position of a Landlord, which is a situation governed by the housing law of the state you live in. You become responsible for everything that needs to be fixed in the tenant's apartment, as well as yours. Although you can put-off fixing of some broken things in your own apartment and fix them at your leisure, the broken things in your tenant's apartment you have to fix in a timely manner. If you don't, the tenant can stop paying rent, summon a city Code Inspector who will list all apartment deficiencies and, before you know it, your life turns into a nightmare.

You must realize first that the simplified versions of a property owner profile are false. It is not that simple and not that easy to be a property owner. You will read a lot of stories about a Landlord and Landlording that happened to me in the last 20 years of Real Estate investing.

Reasons to Get into Real Estate

So, what are the reasons to get involved and invest in Real Estate? There are several reasons and I will list the most important ones:

1. You will make money.

After you invest some money and buy a property, you will be making money in several ways:

a) Appreciation of the property over the years; the property increases in value and you could sell it for more money.

b) If you have another steady job, you will be able to take tax deductions and pay much less in taxes on your income. You will be able to deduct interest payments on your loan and money you spent on improvements of the property.

2. The money will be coming steadily.

The tax deductions and appreciation of the property will be consistent over a longer period of time. If the property involves several rent able units, you will steadily be getting income through the form of rents.

3. The investment is safe provided you do the right things.

You have to be sure your property, which is your investment, is insured. You have to have Fire Insurance and Liability Insurance to be covered in case of an accidental fire, or in case somebody slips and falls at your property and decides to sue you. In addition, you have to take care of the property, manage it properly and try to avoid situations, which could happen, as this book will show through true stories.

4. You can become wealthy and independent.

After you obtain a number of rental properties, you will be able to make enough money off of rents and not depend on your job. The Real Estate will become your job and your profession. You will be able to hire people to help you manage your property so you can concentrate on other things, take some time off and take vacations as you please. You become as they say "your own boss." However you have to make sure you are on top of things; always keep in mind that you are the best and most reliable manager of your properties and your investments. Some stories in this book will show you what could happen if you let other people take care of your property without your supervision.

5. You could become a Millionaire, sky is the limit

If you set your goals and set your mind to do that goal, you could go a long way. You have to do the right things but you have to have a little luck too. You have to be at the right place at the right time to be able to get some "good deals." The more you buy and sell, the more you work at it, increases your chances of going a longer way and becoming a Millionaire.

6. You will feel good about your investment.

Any time you walk by your investment property, you will see the construction, you will see the bricks the foundation and the people and businesses living and working in it. You will realize how "Real" this property is and how safe your money is. You will feel proud of your investment. You will feel that your money investment is safer this way than being in for instance Stock Market, which could tumble any day Mr. Greenspan gets up on his left foot.

What this Book Covers – How Real It Is

This book will give you guidelines on how to get into Real Estate and what to do once you become a Landlord and Real Estate Entrepreneur, as I am. Guidelines for managing your investment property will be presented, together with various forms, notices and other paperwork that you will be able to use in the future for yourself. Some of the forms and notices you will have to modify to your liking and needs depending on the kind of property you have and the state you live in.

The main purpose of this book is to present the reality of investing in Real Estate. It will show you how investing in Real Estate really happens, where and how you can usually find money for purchase of the property and what are the characteristics of Home Mortgages and Commercial Mortgages. Various forms of so-called "creative financing" will also be devoted considerable space. A chapter is devoted to explain in layman's terms what the different kind of mortgages are and how "creative financing" could help if applied properly at the right time and place. This reality of investing is supported by true stories that I experienced investing in properties, managing properties, obtaining loans from Banks and Commercial Lenders and getting "creative financing" in cases where they were most suitable.

A personal experience with a Commercial Lender will be pictorially presented, in the form of a true story with a happy ending for the investor, this writer. The story is very educational and the reader should enjoy it and learn from it. The events presented in this story contributed greatly to my financial independence today.

The "Get Rich Schemes in Real Estate" is included as a chapter to show how other books and seminars tell that Real Estate Investing can work. The critical look at those schemes shows you what to beware of and what to look for to realize any of them. True stories of some of these schemes are given later in this book from my personal experience.

This book will show you through a number of short true stories, based on personal experience, what a landlord's job really is and various idiosyncrasies that happen in his daily life. All the stories will have some morals attached to them at the end, advising the readers what should have been done or what should be done in the future. Stories are given about Landlord and Manager relationships, Landlord and Tenant relationships, Landlord and Contractor relationships and Investor and Lender relationships. Most of the stories are so strange that you have to laugh while reading them, even though the landlord didn't feel at the time that it was a laughing matter. The reader should laugh and be sure that he does not make same mistakes in his future landlord-tenant dealings and dealings with other parties as mentioned.

CHAPTER 2

Get Rich Schemes in Real Estate

Many books and many authors have written about how to get rich in Real Estate Investing. I do not want to discourage you from trying these schemes and principles and I will list some of them here. Some of the schemes will be supported with my own experience, giving you my stories with a moral to each story. This will be the biggest difference here because you will be able to read about a real story associated with some of those get rich principles.

You have to realize why these get rich principles were thought out in the first place. Most of the time people that read these books have a hard time making and saving enough money to have a down payment on their first investment property. Whether you are one of those people or not, you can and should try these methods. However, if you have a good paying steady job, you could make and save in a short enough time a few thousand dollars necessary for a first investment, which to me is a surer alternative. Using Other People's Money (OPM) is always something to keep in mind, but some amount of money will still end up being your money that you will have to put at risk. Anyway, here are the Get Rich Schemes, which you can find in many other books in more detail.

Finding a motivated or desperate Seller

This is the hardest and most important part of getting rich in Real Estate and I agree with it 100%. Sometimes you could find good deals in real estate with owners that do not appear desperate or anxious but those are few and unpredictable.

How do you know the Seller is anxious to sell or desperate to sell? How do you find that kind of Seller? You might see that the property is neglected, there is trash in the yard and neighbors or tenants tell you that the owner is trying to sell. You might find out from the legal ads that the property will be auctioned off in foreclosure proceedings because of non-payment of debt. The owner might hint to you that he needs to sell because he has to pay taxes on April 15, or he is getting divorced and would like to get quick cash before the divorce. Also a real estate agent might tell you about the client who is desperate to sell his property.

Needless to say, finding a motivated seller is the most important step toward getting a good deal on the property. This seller will be more open to various offers which at least promise him that he will be able to get rid of the property and move on with his life.

Getting Control of the property without Buying

This technique can work theoretically and some books talk about it. The first prerequisite for this to work is to have an anxious or motivated seller. The other possibility is that the seller is from out of state, has neglected his property for a while, would like to get rid of it by any means, is careless when signing a Purchase and Sale agreement, or is just plain stupid. Well, if you do find a Seller in this category (I would never be one like that and I have been anxious to sell in the past), there are two ways that you can get control of the property, and both ways include having a suitable Purchase and Sale Agreement with this motivated Seller:

(1) You sign a Purchase and Sale Agreement with this Seller. For example you buy a property for $100,000, giving a low down payment of $1000, promising to pay the rest of it at the closing 2 or 3 months later, subject to obtaining financing from a lender. You get control of the property for those 2 to 3 months without buying it. These 2 to 3 months you advertise and look for a suitable buyer to buy

this property for say $105,000. If the property needed extensive improvements, you find a Buyer who is a Contractor, who is glad to give you an extra $5000 for this house, because this is exactly what he was looking for. You end up making $5000 without lifting a hammer or a paintbrush. However, you do have to have all the other conditions right (motivated, careless or stupid seller) and a suitable buyer, which comes along after you already have control of the property.

(2) You sign a Purchase and Sale Agreement with this Seller. For example you buy a property for $100,000, giving a low down payment of $1000 to $2000, renting the property for $750/month for 12 to 24 months, promising to pay the rest of it at the closing 12 to 24 months later, subject to obtaining financing from a lender. You should have in the agreement that for example at least $250/month of the $750/month rent will be counted as money payments toward the purchase price of the property of $100,000 at the Contract end. Now you find a suitable Buyer, who will sub-lease it from you for $850/month and buy it for $105,000 when the Contract is up, 12 to 24 months later, with only $200/month counted toward the purchase price of the house. This appears to be a very safe and sure way to make money and it could work, provided you find:

(a) An anxious and careless Seller, who will not list in your agreement that sub-leasing is not allowed.

(b) You find a young couple with small children and poor credit history that are willing to rent your house for $850 per month and buy it at the end of Contract, when their credit rating improves.

I had a similar Contract on a property; a single-family house that I used to live in and I owned it. I was the Seller, and the Buyer was Reverend Hardy, who rented to own, but defaulted on both, renting and buying. His story is given in this book under the heading "Reverend Hardy" which you will enjoy reading. He happened to be one of the people who read books on "How to get Rich in Real Estate."

Offering a "Rent to Own" Contract for a Property you Control or Own

This technique you apply after you get control of the property (as already mentioned above). For example, you have just leased a property from an anxious and stupid Seller without a clause "sub-leasing is not allowed without Owner's consent." The price for example was: the Purchase Price of $80,000, rent at $600/month ($200/month counting toward the Purchase Price) + $1200 down payment on the Purchase Price of the house which you have to buy 24 months later.

You can now sub-lease this house, contract it to another Buyer as "Rent to Own" for example for $700/month ($150/month counting toward purchase price) + $1400 down payment, with a Purchase Price of $90,000.

There is your profit, $10,000 in the difference between your purchase price and the purchase price of your Buyer, $100/month difference in lease amount during the 24 months when your buyer or you have to exercise the Contract and buy the house. If everything works out and your Buyer buys the house at the end of 24 months, you made a lot of money without ever buying a property. Doesn't this sound great?

Yes, it does, but all 3 things have to happen: (1) Your seller is very anxious and careless and lets you get control of his property without a clause **sub leasing not allowed**; (2) You find a right

Buyer who doesn't mind paying a higher price for the house and higher monthly rental amounts; (3) Your Buyer turns out good after the Lease Period expires, obtains financing and buys the house.

A similar scheme is much easier if you own the house and don't mind waiting a year or two for your money. You can give it to a family under the "Rent to Own" contract, collect down payment of for example $1400, collect rents for 12 to 24 months, $700/month for a Purchase price of $90,000, $150/month counting toward purchase price. You have to make sure that the rental amount is higher than the monthly mortgage you are paying for the house. You have made out by collecting rents for the entire period and still making your money at the end by selling the house. However, if the house value appreciates during the 12 to 24 months to approximately $100,000, you have lost a little, but at least you collected rents.

I had a very similar contract on a house I owned. I gave it to a family with 3 children on a Contract "Rent to Own," with contract expiring in two years. This was the same house that "Reverend Hardy" wanted to buy from me earlier. This story is very funny and educational and happened to work out well for me. The story is given in this book under the heading "The Brody Bunch." I am sure you will laugh and enjoy reading it.

Flipping Contracts on Properties that you gained Control over

This technique is again possible and appears to be a combination of the techniques above. You are supposed to find a suitable Seller again, who will allow you to get a Contract to buy or rent with a certain amount of money. This contract has to be written in such a way that will give you time to look for a buyer, without having to pay the purchase price. Then, you have to find a buyer, who is willing to pay you a higher price for the property than you paid. Needless to say, both tasks of finding a Seller (anxious and stupid) and finding a buyer with poor credit who is glad to buy it from you at a higher price, even though you don't own it but you control it, are two very hard tasks. I mentioned that the buyer has to have poor credit; because that is the reason he would come to you, instead of going to other properties. You are supposed to be the "Buyer's Savior," because you will offer him a deal that nobody else would, and you would find financing for him when everybody else has rejected him. You have to have contacts with banks and commercial lenders, to be able to do this, and this takes time. I do not practice "Flipping Contracts" but you could try it and do well with it. Keep in mind; you have to be at the right place at the right time.

CHAPTER 3

Buying an income property – a Real Process

So, you are ready to buy an income property. You have to have at least 5% cash down, if you are buying a 2 to 4 family house and plan on living in it. If you want to buy a multiple unit building, you will need about 20% down in cash or some of it in collateral (equity in existing house). There are exceptions, of course, buying with very little or no money down. But those cases are really special, and can be listed and summarized as follows:

1. Owner desperate
2. Owner anxious

There are other cases where you don't have to put 10 to 20 % down, but the 2 above are most common. Of course, if you already own 2 or 3 properties, you can take out some additional money from equity in the properties you own and use that money as a down payment on a new property. Does that mean you are buying a new property with no money? Not really! The equity you took out from your existing properties is your hard earned money! Putting that money down on a new property is a new risk all over again, and that new property has to start making you money, otherwise you will start losing money.

The purpose of this discussion was to show you the reality of investing, so you don't get carried away like those people who follow advice of a myriad of financial and real estate experts. Those experts try to show you how to buy properties with no money down, keep on buying and selling and become a millionaire! You may not realize that those "experts" made some money in Real Estate, but some of their millions were made doing promotions and selling their books. Their schemes and advices should be taken with a great caution. Remember always:

1. There is no "free lunch."

2. Buying property with no money down is usually an exception of some kind.

3. For any scheme or venture to succeed you have to be at the right place at the right time. Keep trying but be cautious!

So the fact is, in order to buy any kind of property, whether a single or a two-family house or a 24-unit apartment building, you will need money in the following forms:

1. Money in the form of cash, from your pocket or your savings account, for a down payment on the property you are buying.

2. Money from a bank or a lending institution, the difference between the purchase price and your cash down payment. This money is called a mortgage.

In this Chapter I will give a brief description of mortgages that you are likely to acquire, what they mean in layman's terms, and how to approach and handle them.

I will also show you the possibilities of "Creative Financing" which could help you acquire property with a little money or no money from your pocket. Doesn't this go against what I just said, that you have to have money to put down, that you have to have money to make more money?

Not really. There are always exceptions to rules. You could and you should always try to apply one of those exceptions to this rule. However, in many cases this won't work. If the deal you are negotiating is very good, you should not lose it by not trying the conventional way, investing your own money.

Financing

Home Mortgage

When buying a real estate property, one needs to obtain a mortgage from a bank or other financial institution. For a house, one to four family house in most states, one would apply for a home mortgage, 15 to 30 year mortgage at prevailing home mortgage interest rate. Most banks or financial institutions would require between 5% to 20% money down to protect themselves against any price variations in future years and irresponsible borrowers, who might want to stop paying at some point in time before the mortgage is paid off.

How is the bank protected? Here is an example:

You buy a 3 family home for $105,000 and the bank is nice enough to take only 5% of your money in cash, $5000, and gives you a 30 year mortgage of $100,000 at 7% interest rate. Of course, you also pay one to two points, which are given to the bank just for the privilege of obtaining a mortgage loan (1 point is 1% of the loan or $1000 in this case). So if you paid 2 points + $500 for the lawyer, you essentially spent 107,500, for a property that is worth $105,000 and the bank is only risking $100,000.

Now let's say you pay a monthly mortgage of $665.31/month for the next 2 years which means you paid 665.31 * 24 a total of $15,968 out of which only $2100 was applied toward the principal of the loan; $13,868 went into the interest payments to the bank.

Lets assume you are in financial trouble after 2 years; you lost your job, had to pay some unexpected medical bills, the tenants refuse to pay rent and you are in endless litigation with the tenants. You decide you cannot afford to pay the mortgage and you want to dump the property and get out.

If you stop paying the mortgage, the bank would take your house back through a foreclosure process, and sell it to somebody for example for the same 105,000. So the bank profited $5000 +$2100 paid off equity +collected interest of 13,868 which is a total of $20,968.

If the property went down $7100 in value and the bank had to sell it for $97,900, the bank would have still made money during 2 years by collecting interest of $ 13,868, which is OK, don't you think? That is what it means that the bank is protected. If the bank took more then 5% down at the mortgage initiation (say 10 or 20%), the bank is really well protected. Most banks also make you take a special insurance on the loan that costs you additional money on your monthly payment, in case your down payment was too low.

How much would you say you lost? You have to figure what you paid for the house, how much your expenses were during 2 years, and how much rent you collected. In any case, it seems that if you stopped paying the mortgage, you would be out a good chunk of money in addition to having your credit ruined. If this was a single family home and there was no rental income, the losses would be even greater.

So the recommendation is that you keep paying your mortgage for the period of years, whatever the initial term of the loan was or until you sell your property or re-finance it. That way you can keep your property no matter whether it goes up or down in value. This rule is simple and is taken for granted by any borrower: "nothing bad can happen to the borrower/home owner, who is a diligent payer and pays his mortgage regularly and on time." Yes, it is true, but this rule applies only for this kind of mortgage, called a home mortgage. A commercial mortgage has different rules; it is a whole different ball game.

Commercial Mortgage

If you were buying an apartment unit of more than 4 apartments, you would be looking for a Commercial Mortgage. There is a big difference. Some of the differences are as follows:

- With a home mortgage your collateral is your house.

- With a Commercial Mortgage your collateral is the Real Estate you are buying, + your personal residence, + all your assets, your present and future earnings etc. (anything that the commercial lender can think of and is allowed to put into the mortgage papers).

- Your home mortgage is fixed for the duration of the term (15 or 30 years).

- Your commercial loan is fixed for 15 or 20 years at the time you get it, but it has a "subject to a review" clause after every 2 to 5 years. That "minor clause" you will find at the closing, spelled out in the papers somewhere and when you put a question to the lender to explain what that means, you usually get a comment like this in response: "Don't worry about it, that review is just a formality, if you pay your mortgage regularly." Usually, at the closing you have a ton of papers to review and sign, so this "minor clause" gets brushed on the side very easily. At the closing you might also feel that you don't want to spoil the good deal that you got on the mortgage and on the property. However, this clause allows the Lender to review the market conditions at the review time, and depending on how he feels with those findings, do the following:

- Call in the entire loan, request payment in full within 3 months. If you cannot refinance with someone else, the Lender can take that property from you and sell it. If the Lender does not get enough money for the property to satisfy the balance that is owed, he can go after your personal home to satisfy the loan. And that is pure business, even if you were the best payer up to then, never missed a payment and were never late.

You can lose your income property, maybe your home too, and the Lender can even try to put a claim on your paycheck!

Sounds scary! It is scary and real!

So what are you supposed to do when getting a Commercial Mortgage?
Negotiate with the Lender before you sign the papers! Be sure that the only collateral for this mortgage is the property itself.

I had a Commercial Mortgage like the one I just explained, and I was brought to the edge of bankruptcy. I could have lost both, my income property, and most of the equity in my house if I didn't find the way to get out of it. I will tell you that story so you can learn from it. You will probably laugh at it too, because I have a funny way of telling this story, even though when it was happening it was not funny to my family or me.

Creative Financing

This is a very broad term and it can mean a lot of things. In general, however, any method that one can think of (and is hopefully legal) to get a sum of cash money that can be paid back to the Lender over a longer period of time in incremental payments could be called creative financing.

Let me try to name several possibilities, in the form of examples, which can all be called "creative financing."

1. You are buying a real estate property for $100,000 and the Lender wants you to put down 20% or $20,000 so you can get a mortgage of $80,000. However, the Seller agrees to take back a note of $20,000 (anxious Seller) allowing you to pay him back that so called second mortgage for a period of years. So, in this case, having the Seller take back a Note for 20% of the purchase price and the Lender financing the

rest, you were able to buy property without any money down, using creative financing.

2. You are buying a real estate income property for $100,000 and the Lender wants you to put down 20% or $20,000 so you can get a mortgage of $80,000. The Seller knows that his property is worth the money since it produces income. Since you don't have $20,000 but you have several hungry credit card issuers, you take one or two of those credit card offers. Many credit card issuers offer "convenience checks" allowing you to write up to $10,000 in these checks and have to pay a promotional finance charge of say 0% to 6% for 6 months to a year, after which the finance charge would jump to 15%. You take 2 of those offers, get the necessary $20,000 to buy this income property and you don't have to worry about it for at least this promotional period. When the period is up, you find another creditor to take the financing at another promotional offer (don't ever allow yourself to pay interest of 15% or 18%), and life goes on. Your income property has to be producing at least as much money as it costs you to pay off monthly payments on a $100,000 Loan plus your expenses.

3. You are buying an income producing property for $300,000 but you have only $30,000 cash and need another $30,000 requested by the Lender. The Seller is not very anxious but at least agrees to take a note for $30,000, but wants his money within two years. Payments on a $30,000 for 2 years, even with no interest, would amount to $1250, which is impossible for your cash flow. Therefore, you convince the Seller to charge you on the basis of a 15-year loan, which at 7% interest, would require only $268 per month payments, but have the loan "balloon" after 2 years. At that time you have to pay him the rest of what you owe from the unpaid $30,000. In this case it would be $27,570. So, after 2 years, you have to find another lender for $27,570 or get it from credit cards as in example 2 above. In this case,

"creative financing" was a second mortgage from the owner with a "balloon payment" after 2 years.

4. You are buying an income property, a 12-unit apartment building with a lot of potential for income at a low price of $120,000. The reason for the low price is that almost all the apartments need renovation and only 3 of the 12 units are paying rent. Since the Seller is very anxious, you might convince him to take the first mortgage, as if he were a Bank or Lender, for $90,000 for 7% for 15 years, ballooning in 2 years. For a $30,000 down payment, (which was necessary to be able to convince the Seller to go along with this), you can borrow from the credit cards as in example 2 above. If this can be worked out with a Seller, you save on all points and credit fees that a bank or other Lender would charge you to give you a $90,000 loan, which could amount to $3000 and more. In this case, creative financing was a combination of other examples, but the main point was the major loan coming from the Seller. This can work sometime, and it does not cost anything to try, with an offer to purchase.

I bought one building with terms similar to this example, and I made money with the deal. The Seller sold me the building with 12 units as described above and gave me a $90,000 mortgage with a balloon payment after 24 months. This Seller was anxious, but he was not desperate. He told me later on as I was paying him monthly payments that he decided to do it for me only, and that if I didn't buy it, he would have required outside financing from any other Buyer. It was something about me that he liked, I appeared to him to be honest and a man with strong principles, which I am. I spent about $30,000 fixing this property during the next 12 months. During this time I renovated most of the apartments, moved-in better paying tenants, collected over $40,000 in rents and sold the property for $150,000. So, in this case I was at the right place at the right time, tried the right offer, succeeded and made money.

CHAPTER 4

You Purchased the Income Property – What Next?

After you buy an income property, the work starts. You have to manage the property. This sounds easy, but is much more involved than you think. These are some tasks that you and some other members of the family have to do, to keep the property operational and the income flowing:

1. Screen possible tenants for vacant apartments.

2. Write Leases or Rental Agreements with new tenants, have them signed; collect security deposits and first and last month's rents.

3. Collect rents from existing tenants, warn tenants who are late that they will be evicted if they do not pay.

4. Take delinquent tenants to court.

5. Have a designated person clean the hallways and report to you if anything is broken or inoperative at the building.

6. Follow-up on tenant's complaints about leaky faucets, broken toilets, lights going out, and have a handy man or professional fix things in a reasonable amount of time.

7. Keep a log, written or mental, of when certain tenants are getting paid, so that they don't have excuses for not paying rent.

8. Pay mortgage, taxes, insurance bills, water and sewer, utility and other bills for the property on time.

These management tasks can sometimes be very easy to handle, but sometimes can turn into a nightmare. During my 20 years of ownership of multi-family buildings, there were quite a few stories that are very interesting and educational. These stories show various things that can happen to a property owner. In order to make your management go smooth and easier than mine did, I am giving you copies of various notices that need to be handed to the tenants, and instructions on when and how to use them.

Management Guidelines, Notices and Instructions

Advertisement for an apartment

A typical advertisement for an apartment to rent would be:

Springfield, 604 Armory Street, nice, large one bedroom apartment, $420 includes heat and hot water. Nice area, no pets, references, first and last rent required. Call 555-3461.

This ad would usually fit into 3 lines of a paper. It says the address, monthly rent, what is included and required from prospective tenants. It should avoid a lot of calls when people asking:

- Where is it located? Is that a nice area?
- How much is the rent?
- How many bedrooms are in the apartment?
- Can I have a dog?
- How much money is required to move in?

With this ad running in the daily paper, questions from the callers should be limited to specific things like central heat, dishwasher, garbage disposal, and most important, how to get an application and apply. This ad would have to avoid a myriad of callers, which are just shopping around. The person who calls should already know where the apartment is located, whether that area is acceptable to him and whether he can afford it. The ad tries to avoid callers, who ask to see the apartment, make appointments, and then do not show up! This happens a lot, because many irresponsible and careless callers realize at the last minute, for instance, that the area was not acceptable or that they have a dog, and they just simply don't show up for the appointment. This is a waste of the landlord's time.

By saying that this is a large apartment, you could explain to a more serious prospective tenant that this means either large rooms with a large kitchen, or an extra room, which can be a study or a very small bedroom. With this ad you try to avoid too large of a family applying for a small apartment, which is usually the case when the rent is reasonable.

When the phone starts ringing you should advise the first time callers to drive by and investigate the location first before they make an appointment to see it. Also, tell the interested parties that you will be showing the apartment on a certain day and time. This way, you will have several parties appear at the same time. Have copies of the application form available at that time, so that each interested party will get one. When I am showing the apartment I usually tell the prospective tenant that I will be checking all credit references, police records and eviction history. When all the parties hear that, people who have something to hide will either mention it or try to explain the circumstances or you won't hear from them again.

Application form

Every prospective tenant should fill out an application form. You should make sure the application form asks for personal data, previous tenancies, employment and income and some other references. An application form that I often use is enclosed. It is a simplified, one page application, which does not require too much time and effort, but provides sufficient information for the first opinion. You could also use a more sophisticated 4-page form that asks about all kinds of credit history and references, but people have a hard time filling this out. With my simple one page form you can already deduce how neat and serious the tenant is, by whether he filled out all requested spaces. The application form is given on the next page.

The application states that there is a $10 or $20 application fee. This just turns away tenants who are not serious. I usually return the application fee to the chosen tenant, but I don't tell him that at the time of application.

Notice also how the application mentions at the bottom that dogs, wash-machines and waterbeds are not allowed. This just avoids misunderstandings before the Lease is signed.

Statement about a credit check is also included. Even if you end-up not running a credit check, applicant will notice it and usually tell you if something is wrong with his or her credit history.

APPLICATION FOR APARTMENT RENTAL (Enclose $20 non-refundable App fee)

Applicant Name   Address   Phone Number   Birth Date Soc. Sec. No.
1.
2.
How long have you lived at present address? Why moving?

Present and past Landlord's
Name   Phone Number   Rental Address   Years Rented
1.
2.
If not employed, state Welfare Case Worker Names and phone numbers
Employer's Name   Address   Contact Name   Phone Number

Monthly income:
Work $/month   Welfare $/month   Other $/Month

Names and ages of people to move in:
Name: years old
Name: years old
Do you have (circle which one)   Checking Acct   Savings Acct.
Which Bank?
Other references:
Name   Address   Phone Number   Relationship

Comments (If no comments, leave blank):

Applicant 1, Signature: Date:

Applicant 2, Signature: Date:

By signing above I give permission for a credit check to be run.
No dogs allowed! No wash-machines allowed. No Waterbeds!

Move in condition of the apartment

You should always make and sign a Lease or a Rental Agreement with a new tenant. An important part of a Lease should be a sheet, which spells out the condition of the apartment including walls, windows, floors, fixtures and amenities. Here is a form that I use:

APPENDIX A (attached to the LEASE)

Statement of Condition of Leased Premises, Move-In Condition

This is a statement of condition of premises rented at the beginning of tenancy. The tenant agrees that he has walked through the apartment with the landlord and inspected all the rooms and items below listed in adequate lighting. By signing below the tenant agrees that the list is correct and complete.
If during the first 15 days of tenancy the tenant discovers an item missing from the list, which is not in proper condition, he should point that out to the Landlord in writing, and Landlord will take steps to correct missed item. If after 15 days the Tenant made no list, it is agreed by both parties that this list is correct, and any damages reported after 15 days are made after the Tenant moved in and took possession of the apartment.

Apartment was in following condition:
(New, Good, Painted, Fair, Poor, Broken, Cracked)

Dining Room:	Walls	Ceilings	Floors	Doors	Windows
Living Room:	Walls	Ceilings	Floors	Doors	Windows
Bedroom 1:	Walls	Ceilings	Floors	Doors	Windows
Bedroom 2:	Walls	Ceilings	Floors	Doors	Windows
Kitchen: Sink	Walls	Ceilings	Floors	Doors	Windows
Bath: Sink Tub Toilet	Walls	Ceilings	Floors	Doors	Windows

Explanation of inadequate item (if any):

1.
2.

Concluded with Item Number ( ).

Date:

Landlord

Tenant

The above list should be filled out at the time of moving in and signing the Lease. You or your manager should walk through the entire apartment with the tenant and hand write underneath each of the items (walls, floors, ceilings) a word explaining the condition (painted, new, good, average etc.). Both you and the tenant should sign that sheet at that time. After that, the tenant has 15 days to come up with his own list of inadequate items. Usually, the tenant does not come up with any inadequate items, but if he does, you arrange to fix it in a reasonable time. This way you will avoid problems later on during tenancy.

Lease or Rental Agreement

It is a good practice to have a lease agreement signed with each tenant. This lease agreement specifies rules and regulations that tenant has to abide by and the duties and responsibilities of the tenant and the landlord. But most importantly, the lease spells out the valid time period and the amount of rent to be paid. A part of the lease, as mentioned previously, is a sheet explaining the move-in condition of the apartment.

Many times if both the landlord and a new tenant are in a hurry, the signing of the lease is left for later. This is an invitation for trouble. Both landlord and tenant should sign the lease and all money needs to be paid before the tenant is given keys to the apartment and the permission to move in. Notice how I separated the giving of keys and the permission to move in! In a few of my case stories, the tenant was given the keys to the apartment but not the permission to move in and that caused trouble for the landlord later.

There are various lease forms available on the market. I have always used my own form, which I have been revising over the years to save me from troubles I have experienced. My lease also gives specifics regarding the building and the building practices that make sense. I would advise each new landlord to make up the most suitable lease of his own. My lease has 23 paragraphs and is presented to you as a reference. I will refer to the paragraphs of my Lease as I explain the importance of various rules spelled out in the lease. My ***Lease Form*** is given on the next several pages.

At first glance it appears that the lease is very extensive and talks about practically normal things that are considered common sense. As you get further into Landlording you will start to realize that many tenants don't use common sense, or pretend that they don't have any common sense in many cases. Lets start from the beginning, explaining the purpose of a lease and the various paragraphs that are in it.

Two very important features of having a lease are:

1) The fact that the tenant can be evicted from the apartment if he breaks any of the rules-paragraphs of the lease. Beginning of the eviction procedure is a 7-day notice served to the tenant spelling out the lease paragraphs that were broken.

2) The fact that after the expiration of the lease, the tenant can be evicted from the apartment for no other reason whatsoever, except that the lease has expired. Beginning of the eviction proceeding is a **Rental Period Notice** or better-known **30 Days Notice to Quit**, or just simply **Notice to Terminate Tenancy**.

LEASE FORM

1. Parties

The parties are the Landlord Alexander B. Brancic and the tenant

Pedro Rodriguez, Age 28

2. Premises and Residents

The landlord leases the following premises to the tenant:

Apartment 2R at 604 Armory Street, Anywhere, USA
People residing with this tenant will be:

Name: Gloria Rodriguez Age: 26
Name: Ethan Rodriguez Age: 1
Name: Age:
Name: Age:

No one is allowed to live in this apartment if he/she is not listed on this lease.

3. Term and Rent

This lease shall be in force for the period starting
First day of March 2001
and ending February 28, 2002.

The monthly rent will be $ /month for the Lease period through 2002 which makes a total of $ for the lease period. Rent is due and payable on the First day of each month to the Landlord or his designated agent. If not renewed, this lease continues monthly with the same or increased rent with all other paragraphs and rules of this Lease staying in force.

4. Security Deposit

Tenant paid a Security Deposit of which will be held in a Savings Account at Town Bank, Alexander B. Brancic and Tenant's Name. This money will be returned to the Tenant 30 days after he moves out, less the cost of damages made by the tenant during his tenancy, the cost of cleaning and any rent due. During the tenancy Landlord reserves the right to inspect the apartment every 6 months with a 24-hour notice. If any damages are noticed during the 6 month's inspection, the cost of those damages shall be added to the tenant's monthly rent, or deducted from the security deposit. If the tenant does not pay for the damages, he will be defaulting on the rent, and proper action will be taken.
Tenant and Landlord will inspect the apartment, room by room before the tenant moves in and the tenant is requested to sign a statement of apartments' pre existing condition at the time of moving in (Appendix A).

5. Last Month's Rent

Tenant is requested to pay the Last Month's Rent at the time of moving in. Last month's rent will be used for the Last Month's rental fee, when the tenant gives a 30 days notice of termination. This money paid by the tenant is not returnable and will be used for the Last Month of tenancy.
In special circumstances, the Landlord may make arrangements with the Tenant for monthly payments toward the Last Month's Rent. If such arrangements are made, defaulting on it will be considered as defaulting on rent payments and proper action will be taken. The tenant promises to pay the Last Month's Rent by the following payment schedule:

(Insert schedule here)

6. Payment of Rent

Each tenant is responsible for payment of rent. Payments by cash can be made only to the Landlord or his agent (receipt will be made). Payments by mail to the landlord by check or Money Order *are acceptable, however a tenant assumes responsibility for mail delivery lateness. Repeated late payments of rent are grounds for termination of this LEASE. Bounced checks will be charged $20.*

7. Changes or Termination

If the tenant wishes to terminate tenancy before the expiration of the LEASE, he can do it by giving a proper 30 days written notice, and also paying for that month's rent. In other words, if the tenant breaks a LEASE before LEASE expiration, this will cost the tenant one extra month's rent. If the LEASE has expired and the tenant is on a month-by month tenancy, the Landlord can terminate the tenancy by issuing a 30 days notice to the Tenant.

8. Appliances

The Landlord does not provide or guarantee any appliances. The Tenant is responsible for providing his own refrigerator and stove for this apartment. If the Tenant replaces the refrigerator during his tenancy, he has to bear all the costs for removing the old appliance from the premises. If the Tenant does not remove the old refrigerator, he will be charged $35 per appliance, added to the rent.

***9. Statement of Move-In Condition** of Leased Premises, Appendix A, is attached and incorporated as part of this agreement.*

10. Losses or Damages Made by Tenant

Lost or replaced keys will be charged $3.00 per key. Emergency lockout will be charged $15. If the Tenant changes locks, he will provide 2 full sets of keys to the Landlord or will be charged $40 for the replacement locks added to the rental amount.

Tenant will use screens in the bathtub and kitchen and bathroom drains to prevent excessive hair, dirt and various objects clogging the drain. If the drain gets clogged-up by tenant, his kids, or visitors, and rooter services are needed to unclog the drain, and take out foreign objects from the drain, the Tenant will be charged $75, added to the monthly rent. If the Tenant overfills the bathtub or the toilets, he will be charged for damages caused to the ceilings and floors below, and for the cost of unclogging the toilet or the bathtub.

Blown fuses, replacement light bulbs and glass broken by Tenant and his visitors are Tenant's responsibility and will be fixed at tenant's expense.

11. Default

If the Tenant does not comply with any obligation imposed on under this LEASE, or if Tenant admits being or is declared to be bankrupt or insolvent, or if Tenant appears to have abandoned the Premises, Landlord may terminate this LEASE by written notification to Tenant. The termination will become effective seven (7) days after the notice is given, except where Tenant has failed to pay rent, in which case termination will become effective
fourteen (14) days after the notice is given. Landlord shall also be entitled to any and all other remedies provided by the law. All rights and remedies are to be cumulative and not exclusive. Tenant shall bear all reasonable costs, including constable/sheriff fees, court filing fees and attorney's fees incurred by Landlord to enforce the terms of this LEASE or to terminate the lease for Tenant's violation of the lease terms.

12. Use of Property

Tenant agrees to use the premises as residence for him/herself and the people listed on the Lease, and for no other purpose whatsoever. If the Tenant at any time starts using the apartment for purposes other than living, he will be served an eviction notice.
Heating: Keep your thermostat at 70 when home, 55 at night and when you are away from apartment.

13. Utilities

Landlord pays for Heat, Hot and Cold Water. Tenant pays for electricity for lights and refrigerator and gas for the stove.

14. Maintenance

The landlord agrees to maintain the roof, windows, walls and doors of the structure in a safe and secure condition. Tenant shall report promptly any dripping faucets, running toilets, gas leaks, electrical malfunction and similar to the landlord, and those will be fixed by the landlord in a reasonable amount of time. Blown fuses, light bulbs and glass broken by tenant shall be replaced by the tenant at tenant's expense.

15. Cleaning and Trash

Tenant will keep his apartment in clean condition. Front apartments will also keep the hallway in front of their apartment in clean condition. Rear apartments will keep their half of the back porch in clean condition. All trash will be sealed in trash bags and brought to the dumpster downstairs. No trash will be held in apartment, hallways porches or driveway near dumpster at any time! Failure to comply with this paragraph of the Lease is subject to a $15 Fine, added to the monthly rent. Disposing of a couch, chair or mattress will be charged $15 fee.

16. Laundry

Use of personal wash-machines in the apartments, second floor and up is not allowed, since they can cause extensive damage to the floors and ceilings below. Penalty: $40 added to the monthly rent each month until the tenant is evicted or moves.

Laundry facility is in the basement; opened from 9 AM to 10 pm. Charge is $ .75 dryers, $1.25 for a wash. Use it and clean dryer filters after use; wipe off washers after use. If the Tenant is noticed abusing machines (using inadequate number of quarters, force-jamming the machine or leaving machines dirty), he or she will lose laundry privileges.

17. Pets

No pets will reside in or visit the leased premises. If a dog is noticed at the premises, Tenant will be charged $30 extra per month from that day on, and eviction proceedings will be started.

***18. Water beds** are not allowed in the building.*

19. Parking

Parking for tenants is on the street. Do not ever block the Driveway! Police are instructed to tow violators.

20. Visitation, Music, Parties

Tenant will not disturb other building residents or businesses with loud music or parties. No loud music is allowed after 10 PM. However, blasting stereo, screaming from the street and from apartment windows will not be tolerated at any time! Tenant is responsible for instructing his and her friends about these rules and making their visiting friends abide by these rental agreement rules. Visitation and/or parties by 20-30 people in one day is a violation of this rental agreement and is subject to a $15 fine added to the next month's monthly rent.

21. Entry by Landlord

The landlord and his agent shall have the right to enter the premises for the following purposes: a) to inspect the premises for damage or needed repairs b) to make necessary repairs, improvements or extermination; c) to show the premises to prospective tenants, purchasers or mortgagors; d) for purpose of bi-yearly inspection for damages with a 24-hours notice. When the repair work has been arranged with a contractor, the Tenant shall make sure he is home or leave a key with a Manager. Failure to comply with this rule will be subject to a $25 fine added to the monthly rental fee.

22. Extermination

In case it becomes necessary to perform extermination treatment, the tenant shall be notified of the time at which the exterminator is coming. Tenant will then prepare the apartment by emptying all kitchen and bathroom cabinets, leave the key with the Manager or stay home for that time. In case the apartment is not prepared and/or keys are not left with the Manager, the Manager or the Landlord will let the exterminator in, and the tenant will be charged $30 fee, which will be added to the next monthly rent.

23. Owner

The building is owned by the Landlord:
Alexander B. Brancic, phone 555-4318
Address: 1303 Amostown Road, Anywhere, USA

Dated this - day of 200 .

Landlord

Tenant

------- *End of Lease*--

You might wonder now, why is it so important to evict a tenant from the apartment? There are several reasons and the most important ones are:

1. the non-payment of rent
2. destruction of the property and refusal to pay for damages
3. Illegal use of apartment

Other important reasons are refusal to live by the rules, causing noise and being a nuisance to the neighbors. I have been a good landlord allowing tenants who pay the rent and follow lease rules to stay in my apartment building for many years. However, there are cases when it is absolutely important to get a certain tenant out and take a possession of the apartment regardless of the cost. I have had a few tenants like that, and having a good spelled-out lease determined whether my eviction process was successful or it failed. Several stories I will present further on in this book will show you how important the lease was and how tedious the eviction process was.

The lease should be presented and signed at the time of moving into the apartment, at the same time when the Tenant is paying all the required money (usually First Month's Rent, Last Month's Rent and Security Deposit). This is the same time when the Move-in Conditions are recorded and signed by both Tenant and Landlord, and the Landlord is giving apartment keys to the Tenant.

Security Deposit and Last Month's Rent

You should collect the security deposit in an amount equal to or less than the amount of the monthly rent. This money has to be deposited in a bank account under your name and tenants name and tenants social security number. After you deposit this money into the bank account, you should notify the tenant about it. However, you would be the only person who has access to this account. If you mishandle the security deposit and you are later in litigation with the tenant, trying to evict him for non-payment of rent, the Court can award the tenant damages in the amount of 3 times the security deposit. Bad or so-called professional tenants will try to request damages in that amount even if they do not have a receipt and didn't pay the security deposit (see my story on Karla). Keep all your records and do it by the rules.

You are also supposed to pay the tenant once a year the interest this account has accrued. If you forget to do this and the tenant complains, you just send him 5% interest at that time, and no penalty will apply.

The last month's rent that you collect you can keep in your own account or in your pocket. That money the tenant can use to pay the last month of tenancy with a 30 days notice to you that he is moving. You are also supposed to pay the tenant once a year the interest accrued on that money. If the money is in the bank account, you pay him current interest, which is about 1%, in the year 2003. If you forget and tenant complains, you pay him 5% once a year- no questions asked.

The lease should spell-out all the rules, duties and responsibilities. My lease presented on the previous pages was developed over the 20 years of Landlording. It gives all the necessary rules and requirements that I would want my tenants in my specific building to follow. Believe me, many paragraphs of that lease were added during my years of management. Every time I encountered a new tenant who gave me a specific problem, I changed some paragraphs of my lease so that the same problem didn't happen to me again. You can write your own lease but I think the lease I presented would be a good starting structure for any future Landlord or a Building Manager.

Notices to Quit, Violation and Informative Notices

During the various periods of tenancy, you have the need to give various notices to tenants. Some of those notices are just informative notices; some are warning notices, regarding non-payment of rents and violation of the Lease. I have enclosed other notices in the Appendix, but will explain their use here.

7 DAYS NOTICE TO QUIT

This is a notice given to the tenant who has violated a Lease, and you plan on evicting him for that reason. The violations should be spelled out explicitly, mentioning paragraphs of the Lease that were violated and the dates when they happened. Here is an example of a 7-day Notice to Quit:

7-DAY NOTICE TO QUIT

September 4, 2002

TO: Lydia Wells
604 Armory Street, Apt. 2R
Anywhere, USA

Dear Lydia:

You are requested to leave the premises you now rent as the tenant at 604 Armory Street, Apartment 2R. You have 7 days from receipt of this notice to leave or I will go to Court and get permission to evict you for the following lease violations:

11. Default You have abandoned the premises on or

around September 1, 2002. You left a message with my wife that you are leaving and left a phone number 555-4104. I called that number September 1 through September 4, left messages for you to get in touch, even though your message on the phone was saying: "we won't call you back because we are leaving! Adios!" After obtaining a police report regarding the incident on August 28 and after reports on the water leak in your apartment, my maintenance man and myself opened and entered your apartment and found that the faucet in the bathroom was left ON and your apartment had no personal items of any sort (no male or female clothes, no personal hygiene items, no toothbrushes, no towels), no items of any value.

7. *Change or Termination By abandoning the apartment you have terminated your Lease without a proper 30 days' written notice. According to this section of the Lease, this brings a penalty of one extra month's rent, which is $420.*

This is not an official, governmental or judicial document. By Law, a Court is the final authority in every eviction. If you believe you are entitled to remain, as my tenant, and that you have not abandoned the apartment, you have seven days to get in touch with me.

You or your lawyer may present your case in Court. You must continue to pay your rent for use and occupancy until you leave. Any such payment shall not cancel or affect this notice.

Landlord

As you can see, this notice contains the exact dates when the Lease Violation occurred, and the paragraph of the Lease that was broken.

14 DAYS NOTICE TO QUIT

This notice is given to the tenant who is behind in rent. It is usually used as a warning to the tenant. This is what it looks like:

14 DAYS NOTICE TO QUIT

September 14, 2002

TO: Patrick Bloom
604 Armory St., Apt 2L
Anywhere, USA

Dear Patrick:

You are requested to leave the premises you now rent as the tenant at 604 Armory Street, Apartment 2L. You have 14 days from receipt of this notice to leave or I will go to Court and get permission to evict you for the following reasons:

You owe $420 August rent and $420 September rent, making it a total of $840 (eight-hundred-forty dollars).

By Law, a Court is the final authority in every eviction.

If you have not received a notice to quit for non-payment of rent within the last 12 months, you have a right to prevent termination of your tenancy by paying or tendering to your landlord a full amount of rent due within ten (10) days after your receipt of this notice.

Landlord

If the tenant does not pay within 14 days, a "Summary Process" form from the Court will be served to him by the Sheriff or a Constable. That form would set up the Court date.

NOTICE TO TERMINATE TENANCY
(30 DAYS NOTICE TO QUIT)

This notice is given to the tenant whose Lease has expired or is about to expire, and you intend or don't intend to renew it with an increased rent. If you have a tenant, whom you want to evict by all means, this is the first notice you should give him. This is what that notice looks like:

NOTICE TO TERMINATE TENANCY (30 days Notice)

January 24, 2002

To: Alba Cruz
Apt. 3R, 604 Armory Street
Anywhere, USA

Dear Alba:

You are hereby notified to vacate and deliver up at the end of the next month of your tenancy, beginning after this notice, the premises now held by you as the tenant of apartment 2 R (2-right) at 604 Armory Street, Anywhere, USA.

You must continue to pay your rent for use and occupancy until you leave. Any such payment shall not cancel or affect this notice.

Landlord

If you would like to increase the rent to the tenant that the Lease is about to expire, and you want to make sure you get the rent increase next month, you could give the tenant a similar notice, stating your intension to increase the rent.

NOTICE TO TERMINATE TENANCY (30 days Notice) with offer of New Tenancy at Higher Rent

January 24, 2002

To: Alba Cruz
Apt. 3R, 604 Armory Street
Anywhere, USA

Dear Alba:

You are hereby notified to vacate and deliver up at the end of the next month of your tenancy, beginning after this notice, the premises now held by you as the tenant of apartment 2 R (2-right) at 604 Armory Street, Anywhere, USA.

You must continue to pay your rent for use and occupancy until you leave. Any such payment shall not cancel or affect this notice

.

Pursuant to the State Law I hereby offer to start a new tenancy in said premises at a rental rate of $________ per month beginning on the first of March, 2002.

Landlord

Other Notices

There are other notices that you should send to tenants occasionally and I have enclosed some of them. They are self explanatory, and are intended to avoid misunderstandings and problems with tenants. For example, here are some of them:

NOTICE *Date: July 3, 2001*

To All Tenants at 604 Armory Street, Anywhere, USA

PAINTING of PORCH and RAILINGS is in progress NOW!
I am asking for your cooperation:

Do not walk in the area covered with fresh paint, marked with "FRESH PAINT" signs.

DO NOT ALLOW your VISITORS or CHILLDREN to walk on fresh painted areas.

Use front stairs if BACK is getting painted, use back stairs if FRONT is getting painted.

USE COMMON SENSE

If You, Your VISITORS or your CHILDREN interfere with the painting and cause damage, you will be assessed a fine or requested to move out! If You, Your VISITORS or your CHILDREN make foot print in fresh paint and then walk into apartment, leaving GREEN paint on apartment floor, you will be assessed a fine or requested to move out with an eviction notice!

Your Landlord

The above notice is self-explanatory and right to the point. It calls for common sense, which on many occasions tenants don't use or don't want to bother using. However, even though tenants tend to be irresponsible at times, they will think twice before they commit any of the above negligent acts after they receive the above notice.

There is also a need for a notice that some work will be performed at the apartment, and that the tenant needs to leave a key or stay at home. It looks like this:

NOTICE

Date: March 1, 2001

Dear Tenant:

My maintenance man or a contractor will come on March 3, about 10 AM to perform work on your plumbing problem. Please be sure to leave a key with the manager if you cannot be home. If you have a problem with that time, please call me at 555-4318 or inform my manager, so a different time can be arranged.

Your Landlord

I frequently use a "General Violation Notice" which lists all possible violations that I can think of. All I have to do is check mark the one that is applicable for the tenant at that time.

NOTICE OF VIOLATION
OF LEASE/RENTAL AGREEMENT RULES

Tenants at 604 Armory Street, Anywhere, USA

Apartments: 1R, 2R, 3R, 4R, 1L, 2L, 3L, 4L (Circle one)

( ) No pets. You have a dog or a cat in your apartment.

( ) Extra People You have extra people, which are not on your Lease, living with you.

( ) Disturbance/Noise You have been disturbing other building residents with your loud music -stereo or with loud parties.

( ) Back Door left open. You and your visitors have been leaving the back door open. Please close it and instruct your visitors to close it!

( ) Trash/Garbage. You are leaving garbage/trash in the hallways or porch, or keeping trash in your apartment. All trash needs to be sealed in plastic bags and placed in a dumpster.

( ) Parking. You (or your visitors) have parked the car in a space where it blocked tenants from the next building or a truck.

( ) Other Violations (list)

I urge you, please, to stop/get rid of the violation within 48 hours. If you don't, I will have to start eviction proceedings, for violation of the Lease/Rental Agreement.

Your Landlord

You will probably have to write some of your own notices, depending on the situation you are in. Remember that a written word or a notice is a little stronger than just a spoken word. Spend time writing notices and delivering them to tenants, because that will help in a long run.

Now, for the end, let me show you a **Note Never to give to your tenant**. If irresponsible and non-paying tenants ever frustrate you, you might feel like sending a note like this. I already mentioned how at one time I had a 12 unit building where only 3 tenants were paying rent. Both my maintenance man George and I were frustrated because some of those tenants who were under the eviction process were calling us every day with complaints about their apartment, requiring maintenance work and renovation. George thought of a Note to send to all the tenants. He showed it to me, and we both had a big laugh. But we both knew we could not send this note without getting me, the Landlord in big trouble.

Here is that Note with some modifications (the original was worse):

NOTE to ALL my TENANTS
(Remember, never send this Note)

January 16, 2000

From Your Landlord

Rent is Due
It is already the middle of the month. Rent is way overdue. If any of you freeloaders have the rent money, cough it up now.

A Word to the Wise
If there are any complaints about your apartment, please don't hesitate to keep it to yourself until your rent is paid up to the cent. So, remember, don't call me. Don't get any crazy idea that I will come and fix anything before I have all the money you owe me.

Contest: Who Can Pay Their Rent First?
The way it is played: The one who pays their rent first in the month is the Winner!
Prize: You get extra time to get your things together and move on your own. This way I don't EVICT you right away and throw your things on the street like you deserve, for destroying my property and calling me and bothering me every night. If you don't move, you will get EVICTED later. So, try to be a Winner, it is worth some time!

Calendar of Events
January 2000 First person to be thrown out is Apartment 2L. Good luck with being a freeloader with another Landlord.
February 2000 and later: The rest of the Freeloaders will be thrown out later, at my leisure. Remember to play my game and buy yourself some extra time!

End of Never to send Note.

Remember, this is the note that you would like to give to your non-paying tenants, but you can't. Do not ever do it. You always have to be nice with them, as if they were the best tenants in the World. That way, you will look better in the Housing Court when you are in the process of EVICTING them.

Eviction Process

Before I finish this chapter I want to give you some tips on how to handle the situation when you have to evict the tenant. This is how I do it:

If the tenant's rent is a few days late, he has not called to explain the reason, and he is a brand new tenant, I give him a 14-days Notice to Quit. Yes, I don't wait a month or 2 months, getting the runaround by tenants. If that tenant is nice, he will come up with the rent after a few days, giving me excuses, like the paycheck was late, or similar. At that time I would also apologize for the note and tell him that those 14-day Notices I routinely give as soon as the rent is late, unless I hear from the tenant beforehand.

If tenant is short a small amount (say $20 to $50), I will remind him of it next time I collect rent from him. If the tenant keeps falling further behind in rent every month and does not appear to be able to catch up, owes me already half month's rent, I decide that I won't tolerate any more arrears. I fill-out a so-called "Summary Process" form, which sets the Court Date and time about 2 weeks later. That form you have to have served by a Sheriff or a Constable for a small fee. Having served the 14-Day Notice to Quit two or three months earlier helps me get the Court Hearing date in 14 days instead of waiting almost a whole month. The 14-Day Notice to Quit is good for a whole year, if the tenant never paid up in full. This saves time and it surprises the tenant! If the tenant wants to pay the rent, calls me and pays what he owes me, I might decide to forget the small fee I paid for the Constable Services. This rule only applies if I haven't yet paid the Court filing fee, which is now already over $100. If I already paid the Court filing fee, I would still take the rent money that he is offering. However, I would advise the tenant that he still has to come to the Court to make an agreement about rent payments.

At the Housing Court on the date of the Hearing, the legal aid will approach the Landlord most of the time, offering to mediate between Landlord and Tenant, so that both parties would sign some kind of agreement. If rent is the main thing in dispute, it is a good practice to make an agreement regarding dates when the tenant promises to pay rent and arrears. The agreement may also include some fixing of the apartment that the tenant is complaining about. In any case, the landlord should sign the agreement, because it takes less time, than to go to Court in front of the Judge. In addition, if the tenant does not pay later, after he has signed the agreement, the Landlord should have an easier time winning in Court on the next Trial date. There could be exceptions, and you will read about them in my stories.

If the tenant is getting evicted for reasons other than non-payment of rent, I serve him a Notice to Quit for 30 days or 7-days whichever is applicable, for the violations of the Lease. If the tenant's lease has expired or he has no lease, I usually give that tenant a 30 Days Notice to Quit. After 30 days have expired, again a Summary Process paper will be served to the tenant by a Sheriff or a Constable, and a week later I would pay the filing fee with the Housing Court. The rest of the Eviction Process is the same as with Eviction for non-payment of rent, except that I would not stop this process until the tenant is out.

When you win the case and the Court sends you a so-called "Execution," you can present that paper to the Sheriffs or Constables and have them physically evict the tenant. However, this route again costs a lot of money. You usually have to pay the Sheriffs about $200 to $500 and you have to pay for the movers with a truck and for storage of the tenant's belongings for up to 6 months.

To avoid those expenses, it is best to try to talk to the tenant about leaving voluntarily. The tenant should be already mentally prepared that he has to move and find another apartment. It is worth being nice to that tenant, giving him an extra week or two to move, so that you can avoid the large moving and eviction expenses that I mentioned.

If you use the lease, all the forms and procedures that I have presented here, you should be able to avoid things that happened to me during my 20 years of landlord-tenant relationships. Further in the book I am presenting various cases as stories with a moral at the end. Read them, laugh, enjoy them and learn from them.

CHAPTER 5

Contractors and Contractor Stories

There are many things to learn about how to deal with the various contractors you will have to hire as a part of being a Landlord. You have to realize that most contractors are independent and cannot afford to spend much time on your "little job." You have to put yourself in the position of a "General Contractor" to make sure all the little details of the project you are trying to do are accomplished. For the renovation that you have in mind, whether it involves fixing apartments inside and outside, rearranging walls, rearranging the set-up of bedrooms, bathrooms and kitchens, you might need a carpenter, roofer, electrician or a plumber. Of course there are contractors that are certified for renovation work and can perform the work of all these trades, but they will cost you more money. The inexpensive way to do a small but complex project, which requires professional expertise in several trades, is to involve one or two of your regular handy men and hire a plumber, electrician or a roofer only for the specific task that your project requires.

Renovation and repairs become very specific and delicate when it comes to fixing problems on the rental property that you own, with a tenant living inside the apartment. I will give you some guidelines and examples.

1. The tenant called you to tell you that one of the outlets in the kitchen sparked when she tried to plug in a new toaster. The spark left a big burn mark on the outlet and the entire kitchen and bathroom lost electric power.

Your action 1 You call your maintenance person and tell him to visually inspect what happened and to inform you whether he can fix it. The maintenance person (or the landlord) takes off the outlet cover and notices that the two wires are touching causing a short in the old outlet. He replaces the old outlet with a new one making sure the wires are properly isolated, replaces the burned outlet cover and resets the circuit breaker (or changes the fuse) for that apartment. While he is there, the tenant points out also that the toilet water is running continuously and one of the bathroom faucets is dripping. The handy man takes another few minutes to adjust the toilet float and change the washer on the faucet. Everything is up and running and the cost to you was about $35 ($5 for small parts, $30 for your or your maintenance person's labor and running around).

Your action 2 You happened to be busy and you didn't do anything that day. The tenant gets mad and she calls the city's Code Inspector. The Code inspector comes to that apartment, writes down the electric violation. While he is there, the tenant points out also that the toilet water is running continuously and one of the bathroom faucets is dripping. He writes down those violations and a few others that he notices (peeling paint in the ceiling of the bathroom) and sends you a letter requiring that you fix the violations. He also requires that you have a certified electrician and certified plumber perform the work and call him when they are done, giving him their name and their license number. Now it will cost you about $75 for the licensed electrician to fix the outlet and $75 for the licensed plumber to adjust the toilet float and change the washer on the faucet. If the electrician or a plumber needed a permit from the city, that could cost you another $35 to $50 per permit. In addition, you have to buy some paint and involve your handy man to paint the bathroom ceiling at a cost of another $75. The little problem has turned into a big expense.

2. You decide to renovate an apartment by replacing the old bathtub with a new tub and shower combination with shower walls, and to replace the old sink in the kitchen. The apartment is empty because the tenant just moved out.

Your action 1 You request a price estimate from two renovation contractors advertising in the local newspapers. Contractor 1 gives you a price of $2200 for the bathroom renovation and $1100 for kitchen renovation including new kitchen faucets with counter top, new base cabinet and top cabinet above the sink. Contractor 2 gives you a higher price, $4000 for the job. You decide to hire Contractor 1. You sign a Contract Agreement with Contractor 1. This agreement should spell out how much your down payment is to get started (usually one third to one half of the contract price). Be sure that the time for completion and acceptable workmanship is also specified, and that all permits and fees are included in the price. Give Contractor 1 one third of his estimate to start the project, which is $1100, since he requested that much to buy materials. When he is finished with the renovation to your satisfaction, you pay him the remaining 2/3 of the contract price.

Your action 2 You tell your maintenance person about the kitchen and bathroom renovation that you want done. The two of you drive with a station wagon or a rented truck to the local "Home Depot," buy the tub, shower walls, kitchen faucet, counter-top, base cabinet and top cabinets and all other required incidental material. You might need to make a few trips with your vehicle, depending on the amount of material the vehicle could carry at one time. Your handy man performs all the general work, including plumbing disconnection if he is confident enough. If not, you hire a plumber to disconnect kitchen and bathroom fixtures at the beginning of the renovation and to connect the new fixture at the end of the renovation at a price of say $150 to $200. The materials cost you about $950, work of your handy person costs you another $500 + some of your time and work. It turns out that the entire project costs you in this case about $1600, which is about half of what it would cost if you hired Contractor 1.

These two examples show you how you could handle different projects of various magnitudes in different situations. Dealing with tenants will make every project specific. You will have to act differently depending on the situation. I will give you a few stories about my dealings with projects of different magnitudes. These stories are real. They really happened and I think they are educational and funny.

Mr. Johnson, the Roofer

The tenant on the third floor of my building told me that there was a leak in her kitchen, next to the window. I used a phone number of a roofer who advertised in the local newspapers. I called him and told him about my problem. The roofer, Mr. Johnson, told me that he could meet me at the building. He said he would climb up onto the roof, look at it and give me a free estimate. I set up the appointment for the next day, 10 AM.
Mr. Johnson came with a pick up truck, which had a large ladder and lot of various roofing materials and tools in it. He was a man in his early forty's with a well-groomed beard and a small beer belly. His helper was a skinny, tall young man who wore a ski hat on his head even though it was already May. Mr. Johnson and his helper climbed up onto the roof and I followed. Mr. Johnson figured out which spot was in the vicinity of where the leak was. He showed me some broken flashings and missing mortar in the bricks above the spot where the leak was. He told me that he could fix the leaks by patching all these troubled spots that he showed me and that he would do it for $300. I asked him when he could do it and he told me that he could start right now and that it would take about 4 to 5 hours. I was surprised that he could do such prompt service. I tried to get him to lower his price, but he would not budge. He said that his material and labor were worth that much and that I will be very pleased with the result. He wanted to be paid when he was finished. I agreed, told him to go ahead and start the job and to call me at home when he was finished.

I went home to do some work and the phone rang at about 11:30. Mr. Johnson was on the phone telling me that he was just about finished. I was surprised that he was calling me so soon, wondering what he could have done in just about 2 hours.

I rushed back to the building and met Mr. Johnson and his helper on the roof about 12:00 PM. They were picking up their tools. Mr. Johnson showed me that all troubled spots on the roof and brick that he pointed out initially were fixed, with some additional spots that he found necessary to patch with roof cement. He wanted his money, the $300.

I was a little upset. I said:
"How come I am paying so much for something that you did in less than 2 hours?

Mr. Johnson said:
"How much time it took is irrelevant. We had an agreement. The roof is fixed; there will be no leak. Because I don't like being called back, I fix things right the first time. Don't worry, you can call me if there is a problem, but I am telling you, you won't have to call me."

What could I do? His words were reassuring, but also the body language of his helper and himself was telling me that there could be physical persuasion if I didn't pay. After all, an agreement was an agreement. I paid him the $300.

A few days later, the rain came heavy. There was no call from the tenant. The next time it rained was the same thing, no leaks. Mr. Johnson really did a good job.

What could be learned from this story?

Hiring a contractor from the newspaper ad could work out all right. Paying a price that is 10 times what it would cost me if my handy man and I did it was my fault. But, maybe I didn't know what and where to look and what to fix. Maybe I gained some experience so that next time I could do it with my handy man, and I wouldn't have to call Mr. Johnson.

Barry, the roofer

I was fixing a three-bedroom apartment on the third floor of my apartment building and I was quite upset to realize that there was a leak in the roof somewhere, making it drip in the kitchen, bathroom and one of the bedrooms. In addition, there was a leak in the stairway section of the building. I climbed to the top of the roof together with my handy man. We walked around trying to figure out if there were any obvious reasons for the leak. That section of the roof was so called "tar and gravel"; the asphalt roofing was covered with gravel rocks. It was impossible to find a tear or damage to the roof, because the gravel rocks were covering it. One would need to remove all the gravel if he hoped to find a tear in the roofing underneath. My handy man and I brought a few gallons of roofing cement and applied it at the places where the walls and the roofs come together and at the flashing with chimneys, hoping that leaks would stop.

After the next rain we realized that the leaking was still about the same. I decided to hire a roofer to fix this leak. I called two roofing companies from the yellow pages to give me estimates. Roofers from both companies told me that they would want to take out the entire tar and gravel section down and replace it with new roofing, EPDM or simply rubber roof, at a cost between $4000 and $5000. To my surprise, it happened that one of the people I called was Mr. Johnson, the roofer that patched up the roof on my other building about 5 years ago. He didn't recognize me at first, but he did remember that we met 5 years ago when I explained the occasion and the building.

He said with a smile: "You see, what did I tell you then, you won't have to call me, and you never did!"

I said: " Couldn't you fix this roof too, without replacing the entire roof section?"

Mr. Johnson: "I am sorry, I anticipate problems in this case and could not guarantee the job. Therefore, I don't want to take a responsibility to patch it, because there is a chance that you would call me back repeatedly, and I don't like that." He was honest.

About the time that this was happening, a friend of mine, another Landlord, told me that he knew of a good young roofer, Barry, who worked for O'Reilly Roofing, but did some small jobs on the side. I decided to call Barry to ask him for an estimate to fix my roof. I didn't have $5000 to spend on a repair at that time and was hoping that Barry could be my savior.

Barry came, climbed on the roof with me and started walking around and talking. He said:

"See these cracks in the brick walls and the cracks at the chimney? They all need to be fixed with mortar, because water is coming in through these cracks and finding its way to the points below, where it is leaking. I would fix all those cracks and also remove gravel from about a 10 foot by 10-foot area, find the reason for that large leak in the bedroom, and I would fix the roofing that is damaged. I will do all that work for $650."

Me: "Are you sure you will be able to find that major leak? How will you do it? What if the roof damage is not in the 10 foot by 10 foot area that you will examine?"

Barry: "Don't worry about it. I am sure I will find the damaged part of the roof and fix all the leaks. Just leave the "how" part to me. I am a roofer, I know what I am doing."

Me: "All right, I want you to do it. When can you do it?"

Barry: "In the next 2 weeks, maybe sooner. I will come after my work around 5 PM or I will come next Saturday. I need half of the money in cash now, $325, so I can buy the roofing material that I need and pay for my helper. When I am done I want the rest of $325 in cash that day."

Me: "OK, Barry. Write me a little note/estimate saying you will fix the roof for $650 and I will give you a check right now for $325, which you can cash tomorrow at the local bank. I don't have that much cash with me right now."

Barry accepted grudgingly, wrote me an estimate saying he received $325 in the form of check. The estimate also said that he would fix the roof leaks for $650.

"What if the roof still leaks after you are done, Barry? Do you give any guarantee?" I asked.

Barry: " Don't worry, it will not leak after I am done. You can call me and I will come back if there is still a problem. But I am sure it won't leak, I am a roofer!"

It appeared that Barry was giving me verbal assurances that he will fix the roof and come back if there was a problem with his work. He was not willing to give me any written guarantee. He also mentioned that he would recommend replacing the entire "tar and gravel" section of the roof, after which he could give me a 5-year warranty, but the price would be around $3800. He said that I should be happy that he was willing to do a roof repair job like this, for much less money, because not too many roofers would do it.

I knew he was right in that respect. The 2 roofers that gave me estimates were not willing to do any roof-patching job, only a replacement of the entire roof section. I was not willing, however, to give Barry money in cash to start with. I felt that a check was a better way of keeping record of the payment. Also, I made Barry give me a short written estimate that he was not intending to do if I had not asked.

Two weeks passed and Barry didn't show up to fix my roof. I called him several times and left messages on his answering machine. It took about 3 messages when he finally returned the call and said he would do it soon. I had already rented the apartment to a new tenant. It was the beginning of June and I was hoping that there wouldn't be much rain before the roof was fixed.

One afternoon about 4:30 PM Barry called. He said I needed to come to the property with $325 in cash, because he was just finishing fixing the roof. I had that much money in cash with me, but I took my checkbook too, hoping I could convince Barry to take a check again.

At the building I saw a large truck with a partial load of roofing material and a large sign on the body of the truck, which said "O'Reilly Roofing Contractors." I climbed on the roof and saw Barry with another young man, probably Barry's helper. They were cleaning up, picking up their roofing material scraps and tools. Barry said that he was finished, that he found the major problem under the gravel and fixed it, among all the other little problems. He would not accept a check. He said he needed cash so he could pay his helper right away and buy some more materials for his next job.

I gave Barry $325 for which he wrote me a money receipt. I asked him:
"Wow, I am so glad you found and fixed that major leak. How did you find it?"

Barry responded: "I found it because I am a roofer." He didn't want to go into any more details. Barry and his helper got into the "O'Reilly Roofing's" truck and left.

I examined all the cracks that Barry showed me the first time I met him and noticed that he did fix those cracks. I also noticed some other areas of the roof that he had performed some work on. I was hoping that my money was well spent, but I could not tell until the next rainy day.

A few days later there was a short rain, which lasted only a few hours. I heard no complaints from the tenants and I was happy. However, the next rain lasted a couple of days non-stop, and the tenants told me that it was leaking in their bedroom. I was very upset. I realized that the water was also leaking heavily in the stairway, almost worse then before. I called Barry several times and left messages, but he didn't reply.

I knew where Barry lived so I came one Saturday morning unannounced and confronted him about my leaky roof. He told me that he was very busy, but that he would come next Thursday at 4 PM and fix it. I came to the building that Thursday and Barry didn't show up. I called a few times and left messages. I also wrote him a threatening letter. Barry didn't respond again.

I decided to call O'Reilly Roofing and talk to their owner. Mr. O'Reilly told me that they would not take any responsibility for Barry's work, because they didn't have any contract with me. As far as Barry was concerned, he said that they had already fired Barry, because he was caught taking their company truck after hours and going to his private jobs, using O'Reilly's truck and roofing material!

Well, that was really bad news. I sent a short letter to O'Reilly Roofing with a copy of the letter and Barry's contract, hoping that they would by some miracle, make a good will gesture and send a roofer for a few hours. I was hoping that they would see me as a future client. It was a good try, but O'Reilly's Roofing didn't do anything either.

Barry never came back. I told my friend who had recommended Barry about Barry's performance and irresponsibility. He said that he would never recommend Barry to anybody again. I hoped that at least by the word of mouth, Barry's reputation would be hurt and that this would be enough consolation for me. I had no intension or time to try to take Barry to the Small Claims Court for $650.

The major moral of this story is that hiring a non-reputable contractor could be money wasted. It does not happen all the time, but it is a risk that one has to take sometimes. It could have worked out all right, but in this case it didn't. I took a risk because I was not ready to pay for the job to be fixed the right way. So I was at fault too.

Edward, the Electrician

My maintenance man George recommended an electrician to use on more complicated electrical problems. His name was Edward; he was about 40 years old, very experienced and knowledgeable electrician. George knew him because he used to work for him as an electrician-helper, and he learned some electrical skills and procedures from him.

One Tuesday afternoon one of my tenants on the third floor of the apartment building called me with a complaint. There were no lights in a part of her kitchen and her entire bathroom. I called my maintenance man and told him about the problem. George suggested that I call Edward, since trouble-shooting and looking for a problem in the apartment's electrical system was a little too complicated for him. I called Edward's phone number and got his answering machine. I left a message that I had a problem in one of the apartments.

Nobody called that evening or the next morning. I called George and told him that Edward had not answered the phone call. George called Edward about 10 AM Wednesday morning and finally heard from him that evening about 7 PM. George arranged for Edward to meet me at the apartment on Thursday morning about 10 AM.

I met with Edward on Thursday morning in front of the building and led him to the apartment on the third floor. Edward checked one outlet in the kitchen, and then told me that he had to check the power in the basement. He checked the fuses in the basement and went back to the apartment again. He said that he could not find the problem, so he had to open up the ceiling in the kitchen and look for a broken wire in the attic space.

I was upset that we were about to start destroying the apartment's ceiling, but Edward repeated that he had to look into attic space. I told him to go ahead and open a two square feet hole in the sheet rock ceiling and he did. Edward poked his head into the attic and didn't see anything that was apparently wrong. Then he went into the bathroom to check one outlet. As he was working on the bathroom outlet, the lights came back on. Apparently, the problem was in that bathroom outlet, probably with a loose connection. Edward closed all the electrical outlets that he had worked on and told me that I was all set. His bill was $100 for less then 2 hours of work. I also had to pay George later to patch up the hole in the ceiling, which had been made for no reason.

The next time I called Edward again was when I had a problem in one of the large vacant apartment that George and I were renovating. It again took about 2 and half days to get in touch with Edward and get him to come to that apartment. Some outlets and some lights were not working. Edward spent about 2 hours checking wires in the basement and in the apartment, with the help of George and me. I told him that I was not willing to open up any walls or ceilings for him this time around. This sounded like a joke, but it was serious. Edward fixed some outlets and got the lights working.

I asked him: “How much do I owe you for this job?”

Edward said, as if doing me a large favor: “Just $100.”

I gave him the money and asked him: “Is there another phone number or another way of getting in touch with you when I need you.”

Edward replied that this is the best way, just by leaving the message on his answering machine. He didn’t give me any other phone number, and he left.

One summer day I had a serious problem with the wiring in the 12-unit apartment building. A toilet malfunctioned on the second floor and water leaked through the ceiling of the store below, causing sparks and the short in the outlets in the ceiling. The storeowner went upstairs and knocked hard on the door of the apartment, calling the tenant of the apartment to shut the water off in the apartment. He said later he heard a large commotion in the apartment, but nobody opened the door or shut the water. He knew that Eliza and her boys were home (see the story "Eliza and her boys"), but they just would not respond. The storeowner was afraid for his store. He called me and as he didn't reach me at that moment, he called the Fire Department.

The Fire Department called the Building Inspectors and me, the Owner of the building. Both Plumbing and Electrical Inspectors, and I, were summoned to the building. The Plumbing and Electrical Inspectors informed me that I was being ordered to fix the problems with a certified Plumber and certified Electrician by that evening. Otherwise the building was to be closed and all the tenants were going to have to be moved out. They shut off both the water and electricity to the building and told me to get on the phone with my Electrician and my Plumber.

Could you imagine my frustration as I dialed Edward's number first and had to leave a message on his answering machine? I had to go through the phone book and newspaper ads calling numbers for listed electricians. I did manage to speak to one electrician in person and he told me that he could come about 4:30 PM, if that was not too late. I told him: "That would be fine!" His name was Bill. I was thinking to myself how it was better to have Bill, who I don't even know, at 4:30, than to wait 3 days for Edward to call back.
Bill fixed my problems that day. Needless to say, I never called Edward again. Bill became my electrician for emergencies.

There are several morals to this story:

You need to have an electrician who is not only experienced but who is reachable in an emergency, through a cell phone or a beeper. In this case, Edward was definitely not that type. I found out later from George that Edward took a lot of day trips and weekly vacations.

The experience that you need from an electrician would help in troubleshooting. If Edward was more experienced, he would have spent more time looking for problems in other places before deciding to destroy the ceiling in my apartment. Also, I noticed that Edward was a $100 person. Any time he came to fix something, $100 was his normal charge. Essentially, if I was to call him one time when just the fuse needed to be replaced, I could expect to be charged $100 that time too.

Jack, the Plumber

Plumbers are a special kind of people. They know that their license is required at some jobs and they know how to charge for that. Also, same as Edward the Electrician, in order to reach any plumber you have to leave a message on his answering machine or his voice mail. If you leave a more detailed message on the phone, letting him know the kind of trouble you are calling about, many plumbers won't call you back if they figure that the job is too small or too complicated with the amount of work required. But the most important factor on which it depends whether the plumber will take your job is his assessment on the probability that he will get paid and get paid promptly as requested.

For instance, there is more likelihood that the plumber will take a job from you knowing you are a building owner than taking a job from a little old lady, a senior citizen, who called him about a leaky faucet in the bathroom.

Here is a short story on the plumber I met. My building was without hot water over the entire weekend. I found Jack, a Plumber listed in the yellow pages. I called him and told him that I needed the largest residential water heater available and that I needed it installed at the apartment building in my city. The reason I wanted the largest residential water heater and not a commercial water heater is because the prices jump drastically, over 30%, when you have to buy a commercial water heater. Needless to say, plumbers could make more money installing a commercial appliance, because they can charge more money. Here is how my conversation went with Jack, over the phone, after he called back:

Me: "Could you give me an estimate please, on how much the largest gas water heater would cost me to install in my building, in place of the one that broke down?"

Jack: "How many apartments do you have there, and how many showers and kitchens does it serve? Do the people all take showers in the morning?"

Me: "I have 8 apartments that this water heater serves, but never mind the showers. I just want the largest gas water heater, a 100 gallon tank if it is available." I knew by the nature of his questions that he wanted to perform calculations and inform me that a commercial water heater was necessary.

Jack: "But the residential water heater won't be adequate if and when all the people take showers in the morning, when they are getting ready to go to work."

Me: "That's OK if some of them will have to wait for the water to get heated. Could you give me an estimate, please?"

Jack replied grudgingly: "It will cost about $700 for the water heater and $200 for my labor. However, if your tenants complain later, don't call me about insufficient hot water."

Me: "Don't worry about that, Jack. Could you meet me at the building with the water heater in about 1 hour?"

Jack: "I can meet you in front of the **Main Street Plumbing Supply Store** in 1 hour, where I want you to bring $700 for the water heater. When I install it, I will collect the rest of the $200. Is that OK with you?"

Me: "Yes, it is OK!" I hung up and called the **Main Street Plumbing Supply Store**, to find out what the heater really cost. The store salesmen told me that the water heater costs $579 and that a licensed plumber would have to buy it and install it. He asked me who was my plumber and I told him that it was Jack.

I was thinking on my way to the store that the plumber was getting $120 more for the heater, in addition to $200 for labor, which would probably take him less then 2 hours. That was a lot of money, but considering that my tenants were without hot water for over 2 days, I had to do it and not look for a cheaper option.

At the store I noticed a parked van with explicit signs on it: "Jack, the Plumber." A tall large man with moustache, wearing a tee shirt and jeans, got out of the van and came over. He shook hands with me, saying: "You must be Alex?"

I shook his hand and said: "Yes, I am Alex. You must be Jack. Nice to meet you!"

Jack said: "I am sorry, but I won't be doing your job. I don't like people checking on me to find out what it costs me to buy supplies. Besides, I am going to a jobsite now where I will make more money than at your job, just by installing two toilets." He turned around, got in the van and left.

I was stunned; I could not believe that the plumber would leave me like this. I went inside the store and told the salesman what just happened. I asked him what I could do now. The salesman told me that he would sell me the water heater for the contractor's price of $579, but that I would have to take it away myself and find somebody else to install it.

I paid and had the salesman help me with it to the car. Luckily I had a station wagon, and I was able to get the water heater into my car and drive it to the building. Over there, I tried to get my Building Manager, Don, to help me unload the water heater. However, Don would not open the door. He was upset about not having hot water over the weekend (see the story, Sally and Don). I had to ask a couple of teen-agers that were hanging around the building to help me bring the water heater into the basement. I spent that Monday afternoon calling plumbers from the yellow pages to come and hook up a new water heater in place of the one that was broken. That was not a very difficult job, and if I were handy enough, I would have done it. Also, if I had my maintenance man George at that time (I got George about a year later), he could have done it with me as a helper. Nevertheless, another plumber came on Tuesday morning around 11 AM and in a couple of hours the building finally had hot water again. This plumber charged me only $120 for the job.

What more about plumbers does this tell you that I haven't already told you? You have to watch not to offend them. Also, plumbers don't like when the customer decides on the way the job is to be done. They like to be in control and they like to feel that you see a Professional Expert in them. Not only does that make them feel good about it, but it also allows them to make more money that way.

You see that having a plumber that knows you, a plumber who has already done a few jobs for you and has gotten paid, is very important. A plumber who knows you would never do what Jack did to me.

Be careful finding a responsible plumber, and do it sooner then you need him. Good luck!

CHAPTER 6

Application Process and Application Stories

There are things that happen during the application process that the landlord or manager should be aware of. One of the most common is the deception by the prospective tenant.

Maria Caro

I was taking applications for a 3-bedroom apartment and checking references. One lady called, asked how to get an application, filled it out and sent it to me. Her name was Maria Caro. She listed that she had over $2000 a month income in child support and welfare benefits, and that she was also eligible for a government subsidy of the apartment. This program is very good for some landlords, because the money from the government always arrives on time. I was seriously considering her because other applicants had questionable jobs and poor income. What caught my eye was that on the reference, she listed my acquaintance Alex Pratt as her present landlord. The phone number was listed on the application, but I didn't call it that day. The next day I remembered that I wanted to call Alex Pratt, so I looked up his number in the phone book and called him. I just got his answering machine, so I left a message that I called. Incidentally, later on that day the phone rang and there was a male voice asking to talk to me regarding the apartment. This is how the conversation went:

Me: "So, what are you calling about?"

Person: "I am calling regarding the lady, Maria Caro, who applied for your apartment. She is my tenant and I am calling as her reference."

Me: "Oh, I see. Are you the manager of the apartments? What is your name?"

Person: "My name is Alex Pratt and I am the owner of the apartments."

At this point I wanted to scream that he was a liar, because I knew Alex Pratt personally and I knew his voice. But I managed to keep cool and proceed with the conversation.

Me: "OK, so tell me about Maria Caro, how is she on rent payments and on cleaning and housekeeping?"

Person: "She is a very nice lady. I had her for 3 years. She always pays her rent on time, and she keeps her apartment clean. Also, she has 3 young children which go to school and behave well."

Me: "Thank you very much, Mr. Pratt, for calling. Since Maria is such a nice lady, I will seriously consider her for my apartment!"

I was so surprised that the person could be so bold to misrepresent himself and give me a bunch of information in another person's name. I called Alex Pratt again and this time I got him on the phone. I asked him about his tenant, the lady by the name Maria Caro. Alex told me that she owes him about 6 months in rents and that she is in the last leg of the Housing Court eviction process. He added that her 3 children, 14, 12 and 11, are in constant trouble, that they don't listen to any authority, and that they have damaged their own apartment and also neighbors windows and streetlights. Alex also told me that the oldest son that lives with her is already in trouble with the police and Juvenile Court. After I heard all that, I mentioned to him the conversation I just had that day with a person who had impersonated him. I asked if he knew who that was. Alex said that he was probably Maria's son Peter, who is 26, and does not live with her, but visits often.

Needless to say, I didn't rent my apartment to Maria. This story showed how during the routine checking of references on the phone, the landlord could be subject to a possible serious deception by the tenant. References should be checked and double-checked.

Also, always check at least two references if not more. If possible, perform a credit check through a reputable agency.

CHAPTER 7

Building Manager Stories

During the time you have some investment property and a full time job, you have to find somebody at the property to keep watch for you, take out tenant's complaints, and report them to you. It would also be nice if the person you elect to be your helper in managing the property is also handy and could fix some things, like a leaky toilet or sink, blown fuses and similar problems. You cannot afford a full time Manager, so you have to settle for somebody at the building, one of your tenants.

There are a lot of people that want to discuss being your "handy man" or "manager," sometimes before even becoming your tenant. The reason is that they want to have cheaper rent and to make some money to help them pay the rent. You have to decide who is suitable for that position and try him on a few jobs first. You should make a point never to promise anybody this job until you know that you can trust him. Also, make the chosen person pay his rent first, then allow him to make money on your small jobs and chores later.

During my 20 years of Landlording, I had a lot of building on site "managers." Some of them worked out better than others. You call them Managers, because that makes them feel good. Just be sure you don't give them too many responsibilities, especially handling your money, until you get to know them well. Here are some of my Manager's Stories.

Sally and Don

Sally was an 18-year-old pretty girl with Italian heritage that lived on the second floor, in the back apartment, with a baby girl. Everybody in the building liked her. Don was 20, worked for different contractors part-time, and frequently visited Sally. He was 6 feet tall, slim, and had a beard. Sally liked him, and after a while, let him move in, to live with her and the baby. I had initially arranged for Sally to get about a $50 brake in rent for cleaning the hallways once a week. When Don moved in with Sally, they talked me into letting Don take care of various small odd jobs at the property for an additional $50 a month. In other words, Sally and Don were going to act as managers of the building, which was fine with me.

During the first 2 months, Sally and Don were the closest to the Landlord, very friendly, and Don was getting a few more dollars for each little job he did (replacing a washer for somebody's bathroom, replacing a broken door handle, etc). However, one Friday afternoon, the 75-gallon gas water heater for the apartments sprung a leak, and it took until Friday night for one of the tenants to tell me that there was no hot water. Don called Friday night about 10 PM and wanted to know when he could get hot water, since he just came from work. I told him he had to wait until I found a plumber. I was hoping to have one by the next day. However, no plumbers like to work on Saturday, so I had to wait till Monday. On Sunday, I received a phone call from Don again, requesting that I provide hot water for them immediately, because they had a baby in the apartment. It was really upsetting to me, because I didn't know what to say. There was nothing I could do over the weekend.

To make things worse, when Monday came, one plumber that I had called in the morning and had arranged to do the work for me changed his mind. He found another job to do! He told me about 12 pm that putting in two toilets at another job would make him more money than installing a water heater (see the story ***Jack the Plumber***).

I had a station wagon and drove to a plumbing supply store, bought the 100 Gallon gas water heater, had the people at the store help me load it into the car and brought it to the apartment building. I knocked on Don's door, hoping to get some help from him. Don just replied from inside, that all three of them were sick in the apartment (him, Sally and the baby) because they didn't have hot water.

I had to ask a couple of teen-agers that were hanging around the building, to help me bring the water heater into the basement. It was already Monday afternoon, so I had to wait until Tuesday for another plumber to come. This plumber came on Tuesday around 11 AM, and in a couple of hours the building finally had hot water again.

On Wednesday I received a letter from the Board of Health requesting that I restore hot water to the apartments within 24 hours. It turned out that Sally and Don have called the Board of Health first thing Monday morning, and had the inspector in their apartment that day. The inspector tried to measure and record temperature of the water coming out of the Bathroom sink! The report said that there was insufficient water coming out of the hot water side, so that the temperature could not be measured accurately. Of course there was no water coming out. The water heater was shut off; it was not working and the inspector was not even made aware of that!

Moral of this Story

Any tenant who you contract to do some work for you, whether for money or for a break in the rent, is after all, just a tenant. The tenant usually does not feel any responsibility for you or your property (exceptions are rare). When things go bad, expect bad actions and bad responses even from the tenant that you gave some special privileges. Good and responsible on site managers are not easy to find.

Any contractor that you didn't know until a disaster happened will try to take advantage of you. You could also expect him to walk away from a job if he feels he didn't get enough money, even though he got what he asked for. Therefore, it is a good practice to have a working relationship with some plumbers and electricians before you really need them.

Managers, Eddy and Johnny

I rented a small, one-bedroom apartment to a single guy, Johnny, who had a job as a social worker. After a couple of months, a friend appeared in this apartment, so there were two of them. The other guy, Eddy, was also a social worker, but had no job. Johnny said that he was a handy man, so he could help me with maintenance work at the property. I allowed him to do a few jobs for small compensation. Eddy, on the other hand, presented himself as a manager. He said he could collect rents for me, find contractors for more serious repair jobs and perform other similar duties. In other words he said he could act like my representative. I decided to let him try.

Pretty soon, however, I had 2 managers (Johnny doing maintenance, Eddy doing management), with my out of pocket expense being only ½ of Johnny's rent. Pretty good for me? Well, it took time to find out what else was happening.

I was too busy to notice, that some of my rents were unaccounted for. Apparently, Eddy was collecting some rents and late rents and not reporting them all to me. Also, after a few months Johnny and Eddy talked me into giving Eddy another small apartment. Now I had 2 guys in 2 apartments taking care of management. It was costing more, but why worry about it when things are going smooth, right?

Wrong!

In February that year, my wife, 2 children and I went on a ski trip to Canada for a week. There was one vacant apartment in the building, and I told Johnny to arrange for a young couple to move in. This young couple had already applied for the apartment. They just needed to pay the required money to move in, which was $375 First Month's and $375 Last Month's rents. I asked Johnny to collect the money from them and give them the apartment keys. I figured Johnny would give me the money when I came back from the trip.

I came back from the trip after one week, and Eddy told me that Johnny was missing. After a few days, Johnny appeared, and told me a sad story. He had collected 2 month's rent from the young couple, let them move in, and then took his girlfriend to Atlantic City with that money. So the $750 was gone, and he suggested that I allow him to do some work for me instead of sending him to jail. It was all a shock to me, but at least Johnny didn't lie or give me a runaround. I allowed him to stay as my tenant another 3 months. He managed to reimburse me for about half of the money, and then he moved out.

Eddy stayed and managed the building for me another 3-4 months until I realized that he was keeping some of the rents he collected from my tenants. When I confronted him about it and threatened to evict him, he stopped paying his share of the rent. Then I had to start with the eviction process and take him to Court.

The eviction process with Eddy didn't go easy. He was a sweet talker. At the Court he talked so nice and sweet that the Judge gave him an additional month before issuing the "***Execution***" paper, giving me the right to throw Eddy out. After I had the ***Execution***, I talked to Eddy, and he promised to move his things out by the following Monday.

That Monday I came to the building expecting Eddy's apartment to be empty. However, I heard from the other tenants that Eddy had never showed up. He spent the entire weekend somewhere else, probably at his girlfriend's apartment in another city. I found Eddy at the apartment the next day. He told me that he had most of his things moved out over the weekend (what a lie) but that he could not finish. He promised to be out by next Monday.

I didn't believe him this time. I said to Eddy: " That would be fine!" However, I called the Sheriff's office and told them that I had to have a tenant evicted. They told me that they were overbooked with evictions and that the soonest that they could schedule the process, when they would give the tenant a 48 hours notice to vacate, would be next Wednesday. I told them to schedule it then. I had another Monday to check if Eddy would come through with his promise and move on his own. Remember how I explained previously that it costs less money if you don't have to use physical eviction, but you could talk the tenant into moving out on his own? This is why I was still this patient.

That weekend nobody saw Eddy at the apartment, again. He apparently didn't move out. I didn't want to talk to him any more. On Wednesday, the Sheriff's office left a 48-hours notice at Eddy's apartment, since he was not home. He was spending most of his time in his girlfriend's apartment.

On Friday, the Sheriffs came and opened the apartment's door. The apartment was intact with all the furniture and some personal clothes. There was even an aquarium in the living room with one fish. Obviously, Eddy was using my apartment for the storage of his belongings, without paying any rent.

A friend of mine and I started taking Eddy's Furniture and other belonging out. My intension was to store most of his things in a small, locked room in the basement, so that I would not have to pay any storage fee. Since this was a small one-bedroom apartment, I was hoping that everything would fit, including the bed with a mattress and the couch. One of the tenants, Carlos, who was also Eddy's friend, offered to load Eddy's things onto his truck and take them to the other city where Eddy was staying with his girlfriend.

I agreed. It was a big relief for me. Carlos took the bed, with the mattress, the couch and most of Eddy's clothes and drove away. I had the locks changed, put a "No Trespassing" sign on the front door, and went home.

Incidentally, this was one of the long weekends, with Monday as a holiday. I received an angry phone call from Eddy. He left a message on my answering machine that he would take me to Court next Tuesday, as if I have done something wrong. I just laughed. I never heard from Eddy again.

Morals: You have to devote some of your own time for management of your property. Other people managing your property are usually inclined to take advantage of you and you should be sure that you know somebody well before you give him big responsibility.

Handy Man Armand

I had a family move into the 2-bedroom apartment on the second floor. Armand was a 70-year-old man with long gray hair. He had a few front teeth missing, wore jeans and a tee shirt most of the time, and reminded me of the hippies of the 60s. He and his wife both collected social security, himself because of his age and her because of some mental disability (she was in her 40s). They had an 11-year-old girl. Armand said that he knew how to do plumbing and electric work, so I arranged for him to be my handy man at the property, and to clean the hallway once a week. The arrangement was that he gets $100 for cleaning the hallways + $10 to $15 for every little maintenance job (plumbing, electrical).

What I realized slowly was that Armand liked to get the money, but wanted to do as little as possible. Every time I went to the property, the hallways were dirty and Armand had an excuse for it: "It was rainy and muddy outside, we should wait till tomorrow." Or: "The hallways just got cleaned a couple of days ago, and I intend to do them again tomorrow." The story was similar with small maintenance jobs that Armand was supposed to do. The job was either so small that it was hardly worth the $15 or $20 that I was paying Armand, or the job was so big that it required a real plumber or electrician. Even though I was not getting much from Armand, I kept him as a "manager" for a couple of years, because I was too busy with the full time job I had. Besides, Armand at least never stole anything from me.

What this story and other similar stories of "maintenance men" and "manager's" teaches you is that sometime you have to put up with less than 100% satisfactory management help, if you are too busy. If you have a full time job where you are making money, it is good to have somebody at the property, which can take some pressure and some management responsibilities off of you.

Handy man Juan

I was in the process of inspecting a building with 11 apartments, and the owner was using his maintenance man, Juan, to show the apartments. However, it appeared that this handy man was hard to reach, especially when you needed him. Juan lived in a 2-bedroom apartment on the second floor of that building. He knew how to do simple maintenance and also steam and boiler adjustments. That knowledge plus the familiarity with the building which I was about to buy, was enough for me to try to retain Juan as a Manager or Handy Man for that building. I ended up buying the building and offered Juan the job of Maintenance Man in return for 50% of rent. Juan accepted it.

As time went by, small problems happened that needed a handy man's attention. Juan was hard to reach. He only had a cell phone and that phone was usually off or out of range. Most of the problems I had to fix in a hurry, so I had to find somebody else because Juan was not reachable. However, at the time his rent was due and I was able to find and confront him, he wanted to make sure that half of the rent was deducted, since he was my maintenance helper. I had to tell him that I don't need this kind of help any more, since I could not find him when I needed him. Juan did at least acknowledge the fact that he had to pay the rent or move out. He ended up moving out of the apartment two months later, owing only one month's rent. Considering the other cases of tenants that I had to do court evictions on, this ended up to be a decent case.

There are two morals to this story.

1. The tenant that wishes to provide maintenance or any other kind of help to the landlord should be made to pay his entire rent first, and then be paid for the tasks he is hired.

2. It is wrong to assume that a maintenance man who worked satisfactory for the previous landlord would perform well for the new landlord. The new landlord is better off hiring somebody new for the job.

CHAPTER 8

Landlording-Management Stories

In this chapter I am presenting stories describing tenant-landlord relationship. These stories are all true and come from my 20-years of experience in managing multi-family apartment buildings and dealing with various tenants. Almost every story has an unexpected twist. Enjoy reading them!

Roger and Marla

A 25-year old single man with a small mustache and a shaved head applied for a one- bedroom apartment. His name was Roger. He listed that he lived with his ex-wife in an apartment and that he had a job as a social worker. His application was very neat and I managed to get responses from his previous landlord and his work, which both turned out okay. I made an initial walk-through of the apartment with him, showed him everything, and he said that he was not worried about any minor damages because he was a handy man and was willing to fix everything in the apartment.

I had to go on a one-week vacation the next day, and Roger didn't have the required money for the deposit to move-in. Therefore, I told him that my manager would take his money and sign the lease with him, together with the required move-in condition form, which is a part of the lease. My manager received the first and last month's rent, and had the lease signed with him a few days later.

Everything went smooth for about 3 months. Roger was late with rent a few times but always came up with it. He was dating a woman, Marla, who was in her thirties.

After 3 months, Roger was late in paying rent again, but this time he started talking to me about how some minor things needed to be fixed in the apartment before he was going to pay his rent. This was a warning sign for me! Immediately, I gave him a 14-day notice to quit. Most of the time this notice is just a warning to the tenant that is late in paying rent.

Roger, in turn, called the inspector from the Board of Health and walked through the entire building with her. At the end, they walked through his apartment too, noting all of the deficiencies that they could find and think of. The lady inspector listed about 25 building Code violations of the building (stairway, hallways, basement, laundry area, porches) and about 10 minor and very questionable violations in his apartment. Among the apartment violations was a hole in the door, which was made by his fist during an argument with his girlfriend. Also, one of the "violations" was that the windows, which were 3-year old vinyl replacement windows, had the latches "hard to reach." The latches were hard to reach, since he was a short fellow, so the lady inspector listed that the windows were defective.

The number of violations was so overwhelming that I had to research further how this happened. It turned out that Roger's girlfriend Marla, not only knew the Tenant-Landlord rights, but also knew the city Code Inspector. She worked for the Code Inspector in a neighboring city, so the connection between her and the Code Inspector that wrote all the violations was not easy to point out. Marla also talked to other tenants, encouraging them to call the Code Inspector too, so that they could withhold rent.

I noticed that I had an enemy in my building. Marla, the visitor to my rent-defaulting tenant, was trying to ruin my business. Luckily, most of my tenants had been living in my apartment for a long period of time and they refused to listen to Marla. Nevertheless, I decided to get rid of her, since she was not listed on the Lease. One Saturday morning about 11 AM when I knew Marla was visiting, I went to the city police, issued a restraining order against Marla, and hand delivered the restraining order to her in Roger's apartment. The restraining order prohibited her from coming to my building.

Both Marla and Roger screamed at me, telling me that I could not do that, since she said she was not breaking any law. I called the police, however, and two policemen came and requested that she leave the building. Marla was upset, and Roger was furious. Their nice leisurely Saturday morning was so rudely interrupted. They both left within 10 minutes that morning, while two policemen and I were standing by. I enjoyed watching them enter the car and drive off. Roger was yelling that he would get back at me.

I spent months getting repairs done on the things that were listed. At the court hearing, the Judge asked Roger about the pre-existing conditions that he signed before moving in. The list of pre-existing conditions was clean; everything was in order. Roger told the Judge that he had mistakenly signed those papers, because at the time of the walk-through, there was poor lighting in the apartment, and he could not see all the defects. Believe it or not, the Judge believed him. The judge's findings said that considering that there were so many violations in the building, it was reasonable to assume that the other violations, listed in the apartment, were also there from the beginning of tenancy. The fact that the lady Code Inspector went beyond her job description and duty and listed everything imaginable, practically requiring a new building condition, was not noticed by the Judge. It was much easier to request that the landlord fixes everything and that the tenant be awarded at least a 30% break in rent. You should notice that my present move-in condition form includes wording that "inspection was performed in "adequate lighting condition," so it would help in the future.

While the building violations were getting fixed, Marla found a "hungry lawyer" who specializes in defending tenants and suing landlords for "infractions of the security deposit law." This lawyer started a civil case against me for evicting the tenant's visitor, Marla, with a restraining order. The suit claimed that this act was in retaliation for tenant's rent payment default, and it asked for a damage in the amount of about $5000. Roger and Marla were trying to turn my life into a nightmare.

It was already time for me to get a lawyer. I spoke to a lawyer who represents landlords and he immediately dropped the restraining order against Marla. That meant that Marla could come back to visit Roger again, any time she wanted. But since Marla was upset with that incident when she was escorted away by the police, she didn't feel like visiting Roger any more. All my other tenants refused to communicate with Roger and Marla, and they both felt like black sheep when they were in my building. After about 3 months, all the violations were fixed and Roger was ordered to start paying rent again or move out.

Roger decided to move out. The civil suit against me was not very strong, because he could not show that he was a "model tenant." Also, since he never paid any security deposit, the chances of him getting some money settlement in this case were slim to none. Roger moved out owing me about two full monthly rents, about $700. With the judges award of a 30% discount in rent since the beginning of his tenancy, he ended up living in my apartment for about 5 months rent-free.

Roger also decided to turn in the apartment keys and have me inspect the apartment at the time of move-out. He wanted to show me (or himself) that he was a man of honor. He even signed a note that I presented to him in which he promised to pay me the amount that he owed me, $700, over a period of 7 months, at $100/month.

I haven't heard from Roger since that day, and I never received any money from him. With the note he signed where he promised to pay, I could try to take him to the Small Claims Court. But who wants to bother with that? If the person that owes you money does not have a permanent address and does not own anything of value, which was the case with Roger, taking that person to a Civil Court is a waste of time and money. You have to make sure you have his address, pay the Court filing fee and then take the chance that he does not even show up for the hearing. You will see cases like this in the stories I present further in this book. As for Roger, I just simply decided to forget about him.

I learned a lot with this case. As I mentioned already, my move-in condition form improved with the words "inspected in adequate lighting." I also learned that issuing a restraining order against one of tenant's visitors is possible, but can backfire if "landlords retaliation" as a motive can be proven. This is why I would advise all future landlords to use caution and proper timing when deciding to take this kind of action.

Karla

I purchased a 12-unit apartment building in December 1999. About 3 apartments were vacant and several of the apartments had tenants, which were not paying any rent. A two-bedroom apartment on the second floor was supposed to be vacant. In January, I entered the apartment 2R on the second floor, together with my maintenance man George. The apartment had a lot of personal belongings, boxes and trash. Two women came into the apartment immediately, to see who was in it. I told them that I was the new landlord and asked them who they were, since this apartment was supposed to be empty.

One woman, with a nice suntan and long black hair, told to me that her name was Karla and that she was just at the end of the moving out process. She was moving into the apartment next door, which was a three-bedroom apartment. She told me that she would remove the rest of her personal items by the end of the weekend. I asked her if she had any money for January rent. She replied: "Not yet!" From the records of the previous Landlord I realized that she didn't pay any rent for November or December either.

Karla invited George and me to the three-bedroom apartment she was moving into. She showed me with pride how she had performed improvements to this apartment, filled in cracks in the ceilings and walls, and painted them. She told me that Welfare would be able to pay me the rent if I just filled out some papers for her. I looked at the papers she gave me and realized that in order to qualify for Welfare, I had to say on it that ***she owes no rent***. I told her that I was not willing to lie, since she already owed me a full January rent.

The next day I gave Karla a 14-Day Eviction Notice claiming that she owed November, December and January rent at $550 a month, a total of $1650. Karla looked disappointed. She shrugged her shoulders, signed that she had received the notice, went inside her apartment and closed the door. From that moment until the court date I was never able to see or talk to Karla. Her door was always closed. She would not open it no matter how hard and how long we spent knocking at her door.

I went to the Housing Court for the scheduled date and time and Karla didn't show up. I was prepared for trial, with receipts and my maintenance man as a witness. I filled out a paper that allowed me to win by default and get possession of the apartment.

A few days later, I received a paper from the Court that I had to go next week, for a rescheduled date, to have trial with Karla. It turned out that Karla came 2 hours late and told the Court Clerk that she missed the bus because she had to attend to her sick kid. The clerk of Court told the Judge, and the Judge decided to give her another chance. One should understand that the Housing Court is very sympathetic to tenants' needs and problems and most of the time would do anything to help the tenant, even at the cost of the court's time and the landlord's time and money.

The previous landlord of the building, Ahmed, told me that Karla never had permission to move into the large apartment. She apparently obtained a key from the previous maintenance man, Juan, for the purpose of cleaning it and painting it. The permission to move in was going to be given to her, when she paid November and December rent. It appears that Karla moved into the large apartment illegally. On the re-scheduled court date in February, I came together with George and Ahmed. Ahmed was willing to help as a witness, since he held the Mortgage on the building that he sold to me.

Karla came to the housing Court and the clerk helped her fill-out prepared forms as an "Answer" to the Landlord and a Counter-Claim. Her "Answer" said that the apartment had cracks in the walls, drafty windows, un-painted walls, and was infested with mice and roaches. She claimed that she paid November and December rent to the previous landlord, as well as a security deposit of $550. She requested damages of $1650 as a counter-claim, which is 3 times the security deposit, for mishandling of the Security Deposit. She also wanted free rents for January and February, due to non-livable conditions of the apartment. This is how the questioning by the Judge and Karla's answers went:

Judge: " Do you have a receipt for the Security Deposit that you paid to Ahmed?"

Karla: "I don't have a receipt because Ahmed didn't give it to me when I paid. He owes me a receipt, he told me he'd give it to me later!"

Judge: " Do you have a receipt for the November and December rents that you said you paid to Ahmed?"

Karla: "I don't have those receipts either, Ahmed owes me those receipts too. "

Judge: " You are claiming bad conditions in your apartment. Did you call the Code Inspector and have him make a list of deficiencies in your apartment?"

Karla: "Yes, I called the Code Inspector back in January, but he didn't come yet!"

Judge: "Did you request the new landlord to fix the bad conditions in your apartment?"

Karla: "Yes, I told him back in January about bad conditions in my apartment, but he never came to fix anything!"

My maintenance man George testified that he went to Karla's apartment several times in January and she never opened the door. Ahmed testified that he never received money for November or December rents or for the security deposit. He also testified that Karla moved into the large apartment illegally, without his permission, since she never paid for November and December.

After hearing all testimonies, the Judge decided to send a Court's Code Specialist to inspect Karla's apartment and give the list of his findings. The Code Specialist inspected the apartment the next day and presented his list of deficiencies to the Court. The Judge took all that into consideration, together with all testimonies, and issued a judgment for this case. The summary of that judgment with my explanations is as follows.

- Karla does not owe any money for November and December rents, because the debt to the previous landlord is disregarded, invalid for this case.

- The fact that Karla moved into the large apartment illegally, without the previous landlord's permission had no bearing on this case either. The important thing was that ***she had possession*** of this apartment.

- Since the apartment had deficiencies, listed by the Court's Code Specialist, Karla is entitled to a rent abatement of $150 for both January and February, meaning that she owes only $800, which is $550 times 2, diminished by $300.

- Karla gets to keep possession of the apartment with a payment of $800.

- The landlord is ordered to fix all the deficiencies before he can charge $550 rent.

- There was no award on the counterclaim, since there was no proof that Karla had ever paid the security deposit. (Thank God for this).

Doesn't this sound ridiculous and apparently favoring the tenant's interest? It does to me and to many other people that read this. Gaining possession of the apartment illegally was okay. Apparently lying about security deposit payments and rent payments was okay too. Refusing to open the door for the landlord for two months, and then claiming apartment deficiencies, was okay even though it helped the tenant's case.

This shows you how very often the Housing Court tends to favor tenants. The Housing Court provides free legal aid and language interpretation for the tenant, provides readily available lengthy forms prepared to help the tenant answer the landlord's eviction process with frivolous counterclaims. In addition, when it comes to testimonies and judgment, the judges very often do everything in their power to help the tenant's case. They look at them as victims of a "ruthless money-hungry landlord."

Luckily, Karla didn't feel like paying $800 either. Living in the apartment for 4 months, and having to pay $800 was still too much for her, especially when March rent was already going to cost $550. Karla decided to move out by the end of March, finally giving me possession of the apartment. In this case I didn't do anything wrong. I was just a victim of circumstances, which could happen to any landlord and could be even worse.

Erica

I considered myself an experienced landlord after having owned a 3-family house for 3 years and an 8-unit apartment building for 3 more years. I had a vacancy in the apartment building, a two-bedroom apartment on the third floor of the building. A young couple, Erica and her husband Jim with a 5-year-old boy, applied for the vacant apartment by filling out an application form.

From the application form, I found out that Jim worked as a cook at Denny's. The form also indicated that Erica, although presently without a job, has recently worked for a Doctor's office. She was "in-between jobs," meaning that she was looking for a job. I called Denny's and verified that Jim does work there and has been a very reliable employee, working as a cook for 5 years. It was a little strange that this couple was living on the first floor of a 2-family house, and wanted to move to a third floor apartment in a brick apartment building. I went to their apartment to interview them and check them out. Their apartment was clean, only their furniture looked a little used. Jim and Erica greeted me friendly.

Jim said: "We want to save some money, we pay here $450 per month, this is too expensive!" (My apartment was renting for $400/month). During a short conversation, Jim also introduced me to his 5-year-old son and said that Erica and he were planning to get married in 3 months. They had the date set. I told them that I would let them have the apartment, subject to them paying first and last month's rent, which amounts to $800, before they moved in. They paid me $200 as a down payment, promised another 200 on Saturday, the day when they planned to move in, but begged me to trust them for a week, when they would pay me the other $400. I reluctantly agreed, and left.

On Saturday morning, Erica called me and asked me if she could have keys to the apartment since she just found a friend with a truck to help her move while Jim was working. I said she could not have the keys until I got the other $200 that they had promised to pay. A couple of hours later, Jim called from work and said he was sorry for not having the promised $200, but would personally bring the money to me on Tuesday, at my house. He asked me to make an exception this time and agree to wait a couple of days, because that is not a long time compared to the long term relationship that we were about to start now! I thought for a minute and agreed. I gave Erica the keys and she started moving in on Saturday.

During the weekend I drove by the building and saw Erica moving things and unpacking, but never saw Jim. On Monday, there was no sign of Jim, and on Tuesday he didn't show up to pay either. I called Denny's on Wednesday and talked to Jim's boss. He told me that Jim had quit his job abruptly after 5 years of working for Denny's and went back to California where he was from. What a shock!

As it turned out, this couple was splitting up and the man wanted to make one good gesture for the woman before he went away: help her get an apartment. I had to be the one, on whom she was dumped.

Well, there was no going back. I had to go to her apartment and demand the remaining rent from her. She had a few excuses: "I forgot my purse at my mother's when we were moving some of my things," she told me. She also added: "Don't worry, the money is there!"

When the tenant tells you that he or she has the money and that you should not worry, that is when you should get worried. The money has to change hands, from their hands into your hands. Until that happens, promises are just promises and you should take proper action, like an eviction process.

Over the next 2-3 months, I had to take her to court for non-payment of rents. One month she claimed that she had slipped $450 in cash under the apartment door where my maintenance man George lived. Of course, George never found any money under his door, and all that had to be explained to the Judge at the Housing Court. Believe it or not, the Judge simply ordered that the money to be paid for the rent from now on can not be slipped under the door, but had to be presented in person, and a receipt had to be written. So, since Erica could not pay any longer by slipping the rent under the door, she had to eventually move out, to avoid being thrown out.

The moral of this story is:

Anything people tell you as a reason for wanting your apartment, don't take it for granted! Take all their stories with a grain of salt! Be sure to check their story and check their credit. Otherwise, you can get hurt financially every time. Also, as I repeat every time: Always take all the money required before giving the apartment keys to the new tenant.

Amy and Bob, Shane and Sheila

I had 2 small one-bedroom apartments which were vacant, one on the second and one on the third floor of the apartment building. Two young couples applied for it, Amy and Bob, Sheila and Shane. Sheila was a beautiful 19-year-old blonde, a sophomore in college. Shane was over 6 feet tall. He was a muscular 20-year-old army trainee with a crew cut. Shane and Sheila told me that they had the wedding date set in 3 months. Bob was a slightly overweight 20-year-old, 5 ft 10" tall with long hair. He worked for Radio Shack about 35 to 40 hours a week. His girlfriend Amy was an 18-year-old plump brunette with long hair, frequently wearing jeans with tight fitting tee shirts, which emphasized her bust. Bob and Amy had a 3-month-old baby girl. Amy told me that she was planning to go to college after the baby was at least 1 year old.

Bob and Shane were friends from the high school and were both CB Radio enthusiasts. From their application I found out that Bob and Amy had an apartment before in another city, but were unhappy with the accommodations and decided to move. Shane and Sheila never had an apartment and were really looking forward to living independently. Both couples seemed nice and were promising to keep the apartments clean and keep out of trouble.

I took their one-month's deposit with a promise that they would pay last month's rent within the next month. Bob asked me if I would allow them to mount a CB antenna on the roof so that they could talk to the whole world. I was not very familiar with possible consequences, and in order to be nice to them told Bob that I didn't mind. Bob squealed with joy. Bob and Amy moved into the one-bedroom apartment, second floor left, while Shane and Sheila moved into the one bedroom apartment, third floor right.

Immediately after the two couples moved in, the neighbors started complaining that some interruptions were coming through their phone lines and that they heard voices and conversations coming through their TV programs. I tried talking to Bob on the phone, but Amy told me every time that he was out. Next month when the rent was due, they didn't pay it. I went to their apartment to request the rent. Amy opened the door and told me that Bob was the one who pays the rent and that he was not home.

Over the next 10 days I called several times and asked to speak to Bob, but he was always out or he was "unavailable." One time when Amy told me that Bob was in the shower, I told her that I would come right over to talk to him. When I arrived, Bob was gone. The neighbors said that Bob left with his car tires screeching so loud that everybody thought it was a police car chase or an accident. I gave Amy a 14-day eviction notice requesting that they remove the CB antenna from the roof and pay the remaining money they owed me, or move out. Amy smiled when she saw the notice; it appeared that even though she was only 18 years old, she was familiar with the notice and the dreadful long lasting eviction procedure, which I would have to go through if they refused to cooperate.

Meanwhile, things were happening upstairs on the third floor, where Shane and Sheila lived. One weekend, Shane got drunk and got into a big argument with Sheila, hitting her a couple of times in the face. Sheila called the police, and two policemen came to the apartment. They talked to both Sheila and Shane, and to make things easier, they asked Shane to pack some of his things and leave for the night. Bob and Amy told Shane to come and sleep downstairs in their apartment. However, Shane refused, saying that it was his apartment and that nobody was going to force him out. The policemen had no other choice but to arrest Shane and take him to jail that night.

Next Monday Bob had to pay $200 bail to get Shane out of jail. Sheila packed her things and moved back in with her parents. The engagement was off, and that was the best thing for her. Needless to say, both Bob and Shane claimed that they had no money to pay the rent now, since they spent the money on bail and the fine for Shane. Besides, Sheila's parents were not going to help any more either. I gave an eviction notice to Shane about a month after I gave it to Amy and Bob.

Subsequently, Amy, Bob and Shane became very uncooperative, claming that the evictions against them were unfair. They kept using the CB antenna until I threatened to call the police and have them arrested.

For some reason Bob, Amy and their baby all moved into Shane's apartment on the third floor about a month into the eviction process. Even though they were not using the second floor apartment, I didn't take possession of it until I had the court paper, the ***execution***, in hand. I felt that Amy was experienced in the eviction process and the housing law, and was looking for a little slip-up on my part. How did I know that? Ironically, I double checked their references later and found out that they were evicted from another apartment previously. I found that out a little late, but at least better late than never. I waited patiently to get permission from the court to take possession of the apartment.

When I took possession of the second floor apartment, I found out that both the kitchen and the bathroom sinks and the toilet were purposely clogged up. In addition, the walls in the rooms had graffiti, the floors were destroyed and the kitchen cabinets were broken. Shane, Amy and Bob moved out of the apartment within the next week, making my repossession of the second apartment easier.

About a week later, we received a phone call from a neighboring state. An older couple had the first floor apartment of a 2-family house vacant. They were checking references of a nice young couple with a baby girl, which just moved from our town. My wife told the couple about Bob and Amy and advised them to rent it to them only if they didn't mind their house being destroyed. We had the last laugh this time.

Moral of this story:

Be very cautious when considering renting to very young people, around the ages of 18 to 21. Check their references beforehand. Keep in mind that the young people are unpredictable and will usually act petty and irresponsible.

Never give a tenant permission to do something you are not familiar with. In this case, giving a permission to use the CB Radio Antenna in a residential neighborhood was a poor decision. After this experience, I would not allow even my own son to use the CB Radio Antenna in our house, not to mention a tenant in a multi family building.

Reverend Hardy

We bought a new house in August and left our single-family house vacant. We had the house listed for sale with a Real Estate broker. Jane, the real estate broker and her sales agent Frank both assured us that selling the house would be easy, once it was vacant and ready for the new owner.

After two long months of paying 2 mortgages and having no offers, we were delighted to hear that there was a person interested in a "Rent with an option to buy" contract. Jane found this client, Hardy, who was a minister of a small neighborhood church in a nearby town, where he was renting an apartment in a 2-family house.

Jane sent Frank to show the house to Reverend Hardy on the 15th of September. The asking price of the house was $70,000, and Jane was talking of a possible offer close to that number, with a rental amount of $750 per month for a period of one year. The reason for the one-year period which reverend Hardy needed was to have time to save some money for the down payment and to establish good credit.

It sounded pretty good to me, since $750 per month was 30% more than we were paying for the mortgage on the house. We didn't need the cash right away, and since I already had tenants in the multi family building, I felt that this would be just one more tenant, and supposedly a good one.

After the showing of the house, a whole week passed, and although we heard from Frank saying the reverend liked the house, he didn't come up with an official offer yet. One week turned into a two-week period, and I almost forgot about it. Then came October 7, a Saturday, the day before Columbus Day weekend. I came home around 2 PM from a soccer game that I had refereed. As I entered the house, my wife said frantically: "We have to go right now, reverend Hardy is at the house with Jane and Frank, he gave an offer and Jane accepted it. We have to go and sign." My wife seemed happy about it, but the first thing I said was: "I hope he is not planning to buy my house with no money!"

Only an experienced Landlord would have those thoughts cross his mind at that time. Any average homeowner, who has been paying two mortgages for a few months, would just hurry to sign the papers, with a sigh of relief. I changed my clothes quickly and got into the car with my wife. On the way over to the other house, my wife was talking with enthusiasm about how we had gotten a good deal, $70,000, what we had asked for. The fact that we would have to wait for a year to get the $70,000 was not important, with $750 coming in every month. Everything sounded so great, but it appeared that the offer was valid only today. Reverend wanted to start moving into the house by the end of the day. I was just smiling and saying: "I hope he has some money to put down, at least First, Last Month's and security deposit, which would amount to $2,250.00."

As we got to the house, both Frank and Jane greeted us with a smile. I was introduced to Reverend Hardy. He was a tall black man with some gray hair. He wore a suit with a tie. When he talked, I noticed that about four of his front teeth were missing. He avoided smiling. We mentioned the refrigerator, the electric stove, the gas dryer, the stove and the window air conditioner. My wife and I agreed to leave all those appliances for the ***buyer's enjoyment***, including them in the purchase of the house. I smiled, as I sensed the clincher was coming.

Jane presented to me an offer from Reverend Hardy and his wife. The offer came with 2 personal checks. One check in the amount of $2000 was a down payment for buying the house, non-returnable if the sale didn't go through within a year. The other check was for $750, for the first month's rent. Jane told me to sign those papers and to take those checks and deposit them at the bank on Tuesday. I smiled again when I was told that the buyer wanted to move in that day, Saturday. I asked Jane if I could speak to her in private.

We went on the side. As I was pointing to the 2 checks, I said: "It does not matter to me who the buyer is, but I don't consider this money. These checks can always bounce. Therefore, if you want me to allow him to move into my house today, I want the check in the amount of $2,750 to be given to me from your office, and I want you to include a letter that you take full responsibility for that amount of money and your buyers check, in case they bounced." Jane was surprised that I didn't trust her or her Buyer. She went and talked to Reverend Hardy again in private, and after 15 minutes, she agreed. I received her check and a letter later that afternoon. Reverend Hardy got the keys and permission to move in.

It was not until about 2 weeks later that I put in a call to Jane, to see how things were going. I heard that the checks didn't clear yet and that she was getting the runaround from Reverend Hardy. After a month had passed, and a new rent was due, Jane finally realized that this was just a tricky professional tenant. We had to take him to court for non-payment of rent. I gave him a 14 Day Notice for non-payment of rent and started the eviction process.

The matter was quite complicated. The bounced checks belonged in the criminal court but that court had a large amount of cases, which were more serious than bounced checks. Besides, prosecutors do not like to take people to court just for bounced checks, because they feel that the case is not strong enough. In this case the "Buyer" could just say that he had changed his mind for some reason. Then, the purchase and sale agreement would be void, and the judge would not see a big criminal violation. He would probably just "throw this case out of Court."

So, we took Reverend Hardy to the Housing Court, but only for the rental money he owed! At the court, he was again dressed in a suit with a tie. He was still a sweet talker claiming that there was just some mix-up with checks, which should be made good soon. However, since it was already January of a new year, the judge ordered that he posts money to the court within a few days. Of course, that didn't happen, so I received the ***execution*** from the court, giving me the right to evict Reverend Hardy from my house.

The execution said that he owed me only $1500, which was probably for November and December rents, I guess. The bad check given for the rent of October was considered a payment, and Jane was supposed to try to get that money in the criminal Court! Good luck, Jane!

In the meantime, Jane had also checked on the church that Mr. Hardy was supposed to be a Reverend to. She found out that this church didn't exist! A little late for Jane, she should have done here homework sooner.

Anyway, Hardy promised he would move out on February 4th, so I didn't want to spend another $1000 to have a sheriff and pre paid movers throw him out. My old neighbor called me the night of February 3rd, around 10 PM, telling me that my tenant had a big U-Haul truck and was moving out that night. I didn't feel like going over there at that time, to check on what he was taking out of the house. The next morning I found out that Hardy took with him everything that was not attached to the house. My refrigerator, stove, air-conditioner and dryer were gone. To make things worse, the medicine cabinet and the toilet seat from the bathroom were also taken. That told me a lot about Hardy. In the basement I found some large manila envelopes with guidelines and notes on "How to buy properties with no money down" and " How to become a millionaire by using OPM (Other People's Money) in Real Estate Investing." I guess those books and instructional materials teach people more than you think.

There are several morals to this story:

First:

Check the references of anybody that will be moving into your property and take cash and insist on cash or money order especially if the tenant is in a hurry to move in. Unfortunately, in this case, this was Jane's job and she didn't do it.

Second:

The courts don't take it as serious when checks bounce in tenant-landlord cases. Courts are overbooked with more serious crimes, and criminal courts in this case would rather refer you to the Housing Court, instead of prosecuting for a felony, like writing a bad check over $200. The same thing goes for a tenant stealing the appliances. The police told me to take that up in the Housing Court!

Even though Hardy lived in my house for 4 months never paying a dime, wrote bad checks for over $2000, and stole appliances from the house on the way out, his only punishment was a Civil Court paper called ***execution***. With this paper, I could collect $1500 from him if I could find him, and if he has any property of value in his name. Makes you wander if you really want to become a landlord?!

The Brody Bunch

I had a single-family three-bedroom colonial house in a relatively nice neighborhood of the city. A city park was located across the street with tennis courts, basketball courts, and a large grassy fields for baseball and soccer. Times were very hard: a lot of people were without jobs; interest rates were high; and credits were very scarce. This house was the house my wife and I had raised our family in. We lived in this house for 12 years. We then bought a modern three-bedroom ranch house in the town across the river. This was a move up for us, but we had to buy first and then sell this house. Well, since I already had several multi- family buildings in addition to a steady job, I didn't mind having my old house as another rental property for a while. I figured that when the market got better, we would have a buyer at a good price.

What happened on the first try was the story I have already told you. This was the story of Reverend Hardy, where I had a "Purchase and Sale agreement with option to buy in the future," with a Lease Agreement in the meantime. It took about 5 months to throw "Reverend Hardy" out of my house, gaining possession of the house again. A professional Real Estate agent wrote this Lease with Option to buy, and the Purchase and Sale agreement. It still didn't work out that well for me.

I started cleaning the house and fixing things inside it were broken. I also advertised the house as "For Sale by Owner" in the local newspaper. One weekend I advertised an "Open House" between 2 to 4 pm. I had to sit and wait for 2 hours and it just happened that nobody showed up. After 2 months, I still had no offer.

One Saturday, I was fixing something on the porch, when I saw my old neighbor Robert, and his wife Dee working in the yard next door where they lived. The house they lived in was a two-family wood frame house in very shabby condition. They were renting the first floor apartment of that house. The house had old drafty windows and a small yard.

Robert and his wife had 3 children, Sue (21), Linda (20) and Robert Jr. (18). Robert worked seasonally; Dee did not. Sue and Linda had part time jobs. Robert Jr. had a slight mental problem and he collected some kind of disability from the Federal Government, even though he was just 18 years old. I knew all of them because they were my neighbors for at least 2 years, before I moved out to the new house.

Robert said:

"Hi, Alex. Nice to see you again. Are you still selling the house?"

Me: "Nice to see you too, Robert! Yes, I am still selling." I turned around and started to go inside.

At that point Robert yelled: "Hey, Alex, how much do you want for the house?"

"Why do you want to know?" I asked as I was opening the door to go into the house. I didn't want to broadcast my price to Roger and to other people on the street.

Robert said: "I would like to buy your house! Tell me how much you are asking for it!"

I knew Robert as a seasonal worker and a beer drinker. We had drank beer together a few times on my porch, before we moved. I knew that he and his family were low-income people, and although they were nice people and good neighbors, I thought that it was a waste of time talking to him about the price of my house.

I said: "You know, Robert, you would have to have some money to be talking about buying my house!" My mother was helping me clean the house inside, and she expected some help. She was calling me: "Come in, son, we have a lot of work to do here!"

At that moment Robert Jr. said: “I have money, I will show you, wait a minute!”

He dropped the rake that he was using for yard work, ran into the house and came back waving a bank savings book in his right hand. So, Robert Jr. and his father walked over to my house and Robert Jr. handed me his Savings Book to take a look at it. I opened it, saw that it was his, and saw that there was $13,000 in it. That was a shock, because I never expected them to have so much money.

I said with a smile: “Well, this changes the whole thing. Come in guys! I will show you the house and tell you about the price.”

I brought them inside and showed them the house. It had a kitchen with pantry, small bathroom, living room and dining room on the first floor. The second floor had 3 bedrooms with a large bathroom. The third floor, the attic, had 2 bedrooms that I was using as an office. I walked them through the entire house, showing them also the old cellar with the furnace at the end.

My mother was upset. I was not helping my mother clean, and as far as she was concerned I was just wasting my time. She didn’t know that they had some money.

I explained to Robert and his son that I had just gone through a terrible ordeal with the last “Buyer,” Reverend Hardy, who I had to throw out for non-payment of rent. I told them that I would be willing to have a “Lease with Option to Buy” agreement with them, for a Purchase price of $65,000. I offered to give them two years to rent it for $700/month, having $200 out of the $700 every month count toward the purchase price of the house. I also said that if they came up with the remaining money any time during those 2 years, the house would be theirs without penalty. The only thing was that I wanted to have $12,000 up front as a down payment, before they would move in.

The $12,000 I requested was unusually high for a "Rent to Own" deal; it was almost 20% of the purchase price. The reason I asked for that much is because I knew they had it and I was ready to negotiate that part down to about $3000 to $4000 if they insisted. The purchase price of $65, 000 was very reasonable, and figuring the possible appreciation over 2 years, they were getting a good deal.

To my surprise, Robert and his son agreed to these terms. They were paying $650 rent for the other apartment, and this was much nicer, bigger, it was the whole house and they would own it sometime in the near future.

I realized that they were very inexperienced. I told them that I didn't want to take advantage of them, so I wrote down the "Lease with Option to Buy" and a "Purchase and Sale Agreement." I didn't put any hidden clauses in these two agreements. I wanted them to realize that this was an excellent deal, provided they came up with the remaining $53,000, whether through outside financing or savings. "Otherwise," I said, "you would lose your $12,000 and all the rents you put in it, if you change your mind or do not come up with the balance of the purchase price within 2 years."

In my mind, I was thinking that if times were still hard and they showed me that they were trying, I would give them another year on the contract. I didn't say that out loud and they didn't ask for it. They agreed to all the terms. They gave me $12000, we signed all the papers in front of a Notary Public, and we saved all the attorneys fees. I gave them the keys to the house.

Robert, with his wife and 3 children, cleaned up the house, cleaned up the yard and made the house look pretty again. They were paying rent regularly for 6 months. The seventh month they didn't pay the entire month. Then one day, Robert's wife Dee told me that they were on welfare again and that I could help them if I gave them a "***conviction notice***." They said that if they presented that "***conviction notice***" to the welfare, the welfare would pay me for 3 months' worth of rents.

Since I was an experienced landlord, with another multi-family building, I understood that they actually needed a 14 Day Notice, which was a start of an ***eviction process***. They knew what they needed, but they just mixed up the words. It was not a ***conviction notice***, it was an ***eviction notice*** that they needed. I wanted to help so I went along with it. It was really strange that a family that was buying a house would use the welfare system to pay their rent for three months. But this is how low income families play the game. For some reason, I started calling this family "The Brody Bunch," because my wife and I thought it would be a funny nickname for them.

After this, the payments of rents continued through about month 15 of the 24-month Contract. Then, an unfortunate thing happened. Robert Jr. did some foolish thing and got into a conflict with the law. He was tried, and sent to prison for 5 years. Robert and his family were very upset.

A couple of months later, another disaster struck this family. Robert died abruptly. He was only 43 years old and he was younger than me. It was a shock. Next month they didn't pay the rent.

During this same time period I had no job. The bank that financed my multi-family building sent two henchmen to conduct a 3-year review of my 15-year Commercial Mortgage. They were threatening to attach the lien on all my holdings, take my house and the other house unless they get some large amount of money (see The Commercial Mortgage Story As it Happened). I went to the lawyer by the name of Szatarra and among other things asked him what to do with "The Brody Bunch" and the contract I had with them. Szatarra told me that I had to worry about myself first. Other then that, he could not help me at that time, because I had too many holdings and was at the mercy of the commercial bank.

I had to act fast because there was a possibility that the Commercial Lender to whom I owed about $200,000 as a mortgage for the multi-family building, would forcefully attach a lien on both of my houses and eventually take them, not honoring the "Rent to Own" Contract that I had with Roger and his family. I wanted to save them. I offered to take back a mortgage on the house provided they came up with another $12,000. The real estate was on the rise again and my house, for which they had a Contract to buy at $65,000, was already worth at least $70,000. In addition, if you count the $12,000 that they paid initially + $200 times 18 months, they already paid off $15,600 of the $65,000 Contract price of the house. I talked to Dee and to a family friend of Roger, Jack, who was college educated and was able to fully understand what a good deal I was offering them. Believe me, I was offering them that deal out of the goodness of my heart. I figured, it was better to help them, because then there would be less for a Commercial Lender to take away from me anyway.

Jack spent about two weeks talking to Dee, explaining how good it would be for her to do what was necessary to buy the house. She was supposed to pay the back rent and come up with $12,000, which I figured she had. However, Jack told me after two weeks that he understood what a great deal I was offering, but that Dee had rejected it and was going to move out within a month, owing me about 3 months rents. Jack explained to me that since Robert was dead, Robert Jr. in jail for 5 years and one daughter already out of the house, Dee didn't have any motivation to buy this house. She would be able to find a smaller apartment for herself and her younger daughter and have the Welfare System help her with expenses. This is how she had lived on and off most of her life, so she didn't want to change that with the complication of owning a house.

This was sad, but turned up very good for me. I regained possession of this house and was able to sell it 6 months later. I convinced the Commercial Lender to renew my $250,000 mortgage for another 2 years (see: The Commercial Mortgage Story As it Happened) without paying any additional money to him. When you read that story you will see what a good negotiator I was.

This story shows you how good and profitable a "Rent to Own" Contract can be for the Seller of the house, provided he finds a suitable buyer. It also shows that the extra money I made on this deal was attributed mostly to the circumstances, the combination of unexpected events and the fact that I was at the right place at the right time.

A Continuing Saga on Reverend Hardy

You thought I was finished with Reverend Hardy? Not really. Reverend Hardy was known to the City Officials and Prosecuting Attorney as a small criminal. So, after a couple years have passed, I received a notice from the Court to come in on June 15 as a victim/witness regarding my stolen appliances and bounced checks. The police had Hardy in jail on various petty charges. The same notice also said that if I don't show up on that day, I would be subject to an arrest! Wow!

So, I came to court. The prosecutor talked to me regarding my appliances and I repeated to them that they were stolen by Hardy when he moved out. Hardy, on the other hand, told them that the case was settled in the Housing Court. What the meaning was, I had the execution paper regarding $1500 of non-paid rents, he never paid any of that because I could never find him, and therefore he considered the case settled!

Hardy didn't admit stealing any appliances and he requested that he has a Jury Trial. He was allowed to have a Jury Trial for the date of October 10 and was released with a $200 bail. Four months later after receiving another "invitation" from the Court to show up for October 10 or be arrested, I came to Court. Reverend Hardy didn't show up. I wasted my time, and didn't hear about Hardy for another 3 years. Apparently, the court systems and the police are so busy with higher profile crimes that they don't bother looking for a small criminal like this, even though they have an arrest warrant.

The system apparently waited until Hardy got stopped for a traffic violation 3 or 4 years later. About 10 years after the crime was committed, Hardy was arrested again for something and brought to Court. The Trial Date was again set a few months later. I came as a witness and we had a trial with a judge. Hardy had a defense lawyer awarded to him by the Court. This defense lawyer tried to get Hardy to plead guilty with no success. At the trial I testified about what happened.

The defense lawyer asked me to produce receipts of appliances that were stolen 10 years ago and bought 12 to 15 years ago. I was able to produce only estimates of the appliance stores, not the real receipts. When Hardy came to testify, he said that appliances were left in the house, and that I should ask the Real Estate agent about their whereabouts.

Needless to say, there was a "reasonable doubt" and Reverend Hardy was found NOT GUILTY. And what about the ***execution*** for the $1500 of non-paid rents? That didn't belong in the Criminal Court, so I have another 10 years to try to collect that. How? Who knows? Since Hardy does not have a penny to his name and does not have a car registered to his name, there is nothing I can do about it. Besides, I was not even provided with his address. Yes, you heard it right. The prosecuting attorney didn't even request that Hardy give his present address.

Moral: Don't let this happen to you. It seems unreal and is very frustrating.

Eliza and her boys

I was in the process of fixing up a 3-bedroom apartment on the second floor of the building. The apartment just became vacant after a 3-month eviction process for a non-paying tenant. The apartment needed walls to be painted, the bathroom enclosure needed some caulking and the entire apartment needed cleaning. A 38-year-old lady with 3 sons applied for it. Her name was Eliza.

Eliza said that she had 3 nice boys, who were 12, 14 and 15 years of age. They were all doing well in a special school they were attending. She also had a brother Alfred, who was an overweight 40 year old with a "beer belly." Although I told Eliza that the apartment was not going to be ready for another 2 to 3 weeks, she insisted that she will pay me the required deposit and rent, and have her brother and her 3 sons help her with the cleaning and painting of the apartment. This was very tempting for me. If I rented her the apartment before it was done, I would essentially get one month's rent extra. She would be paying me for the time I would have spent working on the apartment.

I made a letter agreement with Eliza, promising to supply her with all the painting and cleaning materials. Then she gave me the deposit and one month's rent. I told her that she had to wait at least 3-4 days until I fixed up the bathroom and the kitchen floor. Although she promised she would wait as I requested, the next day there was a U-Haul truck in front of the building. Alfred, the 3 boys and another men who Eliza called "her fiancée," were all working on moving the furniture. The front door of the apartment was removed and set on the side and the front door of the apartment building was propped wide open.

I was surprised and upset too. I asked Eliza if she remembered the promise in her agreement to wait. She told me not to worry about it. They would all work on fixing the rest of the things in the apartment. I didn't want a big fight right at the beginning of her tenancy, so I let it go. In the following days I managed to come in with my maintenance men George, to fix the kitchen floor and the bathroom. However, the fact that tenants were already inside and didn't want to be disturbed was hampering things.

What started happening was a big headache for my maintenance man and myself. Eliza started behaving like she was the supreme boss and everything revolved around her. When George came at 9 AM to knock on her apartment door, trying to get in (as pre-arranged) to fix the bathroom and kitchen problems, she would not open the door. Then about 11 AM she would call George and me asking why we were not in her apartment, fixing things: she was good and ready then! Trying to explain to her that everybody has a schedule, and that she should coordinate her schedule with ours, was impossible.

In future weeks, George managed to get inside her apartment to fix a few things, but some bathroom issues (chipped paint on the walls) were not completed because Eliza said that she and her sons would finish them at their leisure.

In the following months her sons started doing very crazy things that affected both my building and my other tenants. The youngest one, Kanu, had a small unregistered motorcycle that I didn't know about when they moved in. He was burning rubber with that motorcycle all around the building. He was also burning the asphalt in the courtyard of my building. When I told Eliza what her youngest son was doing, she told me that I was mistaken and that somebody else must have burned holes in my asphalt courtyard. I had witnesses that had seen him do it, but there was no point in arguing with Eliza.

In addition, Kanu was working on his motorcycle on a daily basis, trying to improve the motorcycle's performance. His older brothers were helping him, but at the end of the day they would leave a big mess in the yard, with scattered parts all around the yard and oil spots in various places. My maintenance man George was warning the boys that if they continued doing this, he would one day throw all their motorcycle parts and motorcycle itself into the dumpster.

The boys practically ignored him, figuring that he could not do anything to them and that he would not dare throw the motorcycle into the dumpster. Unfortunately, they were right. George's warning was nothing more than a threat. The motorcycle was too big to lift and fit into the dumpster.

I was just debating on what I could legally do against her son who was not 13 yet, when I received another complaint about her other boy. Josh (14) supposedly got in an argument with another tenant's daughter (14). Josh threw eggs and tomatoes at the girl and her windows and left big stains on her windows. When I tried to tell Eliza what her other boy did to the neighbor's window, she told me that the girl was the one who actually did it, and not her nice boy.

About four months after Eliza moved in, I rented a two-bedroom apartment to a middle-aged couple, Patty and Sammy. The back of their apartment was facing the yard, where Eliza's boys were working on the motorcycle on a daily basis. As Patty and Sam moved in, they brought their things in their beautiful late model Lincoln Continental. They left the car parked that first night in the courtyard, facing their back porch and the kitchen window. In the morning, the passenger side window of the Lincoln had been broken with a brick and the stereo system was missing. Patty and Sam were upset; the police came to take their statement and pictures. The policemen asked if anybody had seen anything. Eliza's three boys were standing at their back porch looking down and smiling, saying that they didn't see anything. George and I were absolutely convinced that Eliza's boys had done it, because they didn't want somebody new intruding on their mechanics shop, the yard where they were working on Kanu's motorcycle. There were no witnesses, and neither the police or me could not do anything.

I finally had to make the decision to start court eviction proceedings against Eliza, because my apartment building was starting to suffer. I gave her a 30 days notice to vacate the premises. With this notice, as there was no Lease, I, as a landlord didn't have to state any reason for eviction. However, since she was about one month behind in rent, I had to say on that notice that she owed me about $600 in back rent. In addition, I stated that her boys had done damage to my property, had disturbed the neighbors, and had also damaged to other people's personal property.

One winter day before the court date arrived, the building's boiler stopped working. I called the heating company, and their serviceman and I both looked everywhere for the trouble. My maintenance man was also there trying to figure out what had happened. Finally, we discovered that the thermostat wire going from the boiler to the roof along a wooden beam, had been cut at the floor level, at the beginning of the porch. As George started soldering the wire, he noticed three smiling heads on the second floor back porches. They were Eliza's boys, her little angels. The oldest one yelled: "Hey, what are you doing down there? Fixing the heat?!" All three of them laughed after that.

What can I say? It was obvious that they knew what was going on. And why did they know? Because they were the ones who had cut the thermostat wire, just to see what would happen. Proving that they had done it would be impossible. However, in view of everything that had gone on, and all the trouble that their family had caused, I was convinced that they had done it.

Hopefully, I would be able to use this in the Housing Court. However, it turned out that the landlord has to have a very strong case with documentation and a perfect building in order to succeed in eviction. This is what happened.

At the Housing Court on the date of the hearing, Eliza came and asked the legal aid for help. They helped her fill out an Answer to the landlord form, a form specially prepared for tenants' use. On that form she checked-off paragraphs regarding tenants complaints on apartment conditions. She wrote in about an unpainted kitchen and bathroom, and about one electric outlet that had no power. Those were her reasons for non-payment of rent, even though she has promised to finish all the painting when she had moved-in.

The judge opened the hearing with a general statement:

Judge: "This is a case where the tenant is complaining about apartment conditions and the landlord is retaliating with eviction proceedings. Is that right, Mr. Landlord? Go ahead and present your case."

Me: " No, Your Honor, this is a case where I am evicting for ***No Lease***. The other reasons I listed were for disturbing the neighbors and destroying my property. My case was initiated with a 30 Days Notice, not with 14 Day Notice for non-payment of rent."

The Judge smiled at me, probably thinking how ignorant I am: "But she owes you rent and she is complaining about bad conditions in the apartment? Isn't that right?"

"That's right, Your Honor!" I replied.

The Judge smiled then and said: "See, this is what I said. Go ahead and proceed with presenting your case."

I didn't dare argue about the type of eviction any more. The judge has just converted it into a simple case of "Eviction for Non-Payment of Rent." If I argued, I was afraid I could be held in contempt of court, or at least my case would be thrown out.
I proceeded to explain about all the destruction of my property and other people's property that Eliza's boys had done. I added that this was the first time I had heard about a broken electrical outlet. I also said that Eliza had promised to paint all the walls when she had moved-in.

Eliza presented herself with a crying act, and told the Judge that she was a victim of an uncaring landlord who does not fix anything in her apartment. She said that her children, the "young little angels," had not done any of those things of which I was accusing them. She presented to the court that her kitchen and bathroom walls were not completely painted, and that she and her family had suffered because of that. She said that she had told me about the broken outlet, but I never sent anybody to fix it.

The judge asked Eliza if she had ever called the Building Inspector to complain about apartment conditions. Eliza said that she had called him but that he had not come yet. What an obvious lie that was.

The Judge ordered the court inspector to go and inspect her apartment. He verified that the kitchen and bathroom walls needed to be painted, that the shower walls had mildew, and that one outlet in the kitchen had no power. In addition, he marked that the bedroom walls had an excessive number of writings and posters which needed to be removed.

The fact that she and her family had moved into the apartment before it was completely ready and without my (the landlord's) authorization, promising that they would complete the painting, didn't matter to the Court. As far as The Court was concerned, the landlord is responsible for all repairs and maintenance, and I was ordered to complete the work. The Housing Court Specialist appraised the apartment, and the rental amount was diminished by about $100 a month from the start of tenancy. It was not possible to prove that the damages to the building were caused by tenant's children due to lack of evidence; there were no eyewitnesses willing to testify. The judge allowed Eliza to retain possession of the apartment, even though I was evicting for possession, with a 30 days notice. I was ordered to fix everything and ended up owing her money due to diminished rental amount that the judge had estimated, multiplied by the number of months she had lived there.

This was a very depressing outcome for me. I sold the building about a month after that court finding and instructed the new landlord about Eliza. I did make some money. The difference between the selling price and my buying price was $30,000, because I had improved the property tremendously over the 12-month period. I had spent about $20,000 fixing the building and moving in paying tenants, so I had managed to collect about

$40,000 in rents that year. However, the selling price of the building was still diminished as a reflection of troubles that the building would come with.

There are several morals to this case and I will list them.

- The tenant should not be allowed to move into an apartment, which is unfinished.
- The tenant should sign a Lease and move-in condition form, spelling out conditions of the entire apartment at the time of moving in. If possible, pictures should be taken to substantiate at a later date all the damages caused by tenant.
- Every incident of Lease Violation should be noted with the exact date and time and if possible police report should be obtained. These procedures take time; filling out forms is a burden, but saves a lot of aggravation later.

If all of the above had been done properly, the judge would have had a harder time converting an ***Eviction for Possession*** into an ***Eviction for Non-Payment of Rent***.

Susan, the businesswoman

I was getting a 3-bedroom apartment ready for rental. A new modern kitchen sink with kitchen cabinets were installed, bathroom was modernized and cleaned, and all rooms were cleaned and walls painted. Susan, a 35-year-old woman in appliance business (so she said) applied for an apartment. Her application said that she was from a city in Mid-West, and had moved from there a few months ago, with her 5-year-old daughter and a 3-year-old son.

Susan inspected the apartment and said that it was OK but that she would not take it unless the kitchen linoleum was completely changed. The linoleum didn't have much damage, just a few cuts, and I thought that she must be a very classy lady. I spent money for the linoleum and my maintenance man, George, and I worked most of the day to install the new linoleum in the kitchen and front and back entry hallways. I told Susan that I was done, and I wanted $1500 from her ($600 first month, $600 last month's and $300 for security deposit). Susan said that she would rather pay $40 extra per month if I agreed to pay her gas and electric bill.

I agreed, but then there were more requests coming. Susan said that she would pay me $740 which is $640 first month's rent + $100 security, but that she would give me the other money (over $900) within 10 days, after she collected the alimony and some business invoices that were coming. I needed the money, since I had been getting this apartment ready for 2 months. I figured that for this classy lady I could make an exception and wait a couple of weeks for the rest of the money.

Susan did move in the next day, and I was surprised when I saw the junky car she was driving and worn out furniture that was being brought in. During the following few days I had to help Susan "jump" her dead car with my car couple of times, so she could go shopping.

Two weeks went by. When I asked for the rest of the money, she told me that her ex-husband had defaulted on the alimony and that she would get me the money from her business, any day. After the entire month was gone, I decided to give Susan a 14-day eviction notice.

From then on, I had a hard time getting to talk to her. She would not open her door when I was knocking. Some evenings other tenants called me because there were loud noises coming from the apartment. Susan and her boyfriend were arguing and fighting. It escalated into him beating her up, and she called the police. The boyfriend had enough sense to leave before the police came, so everything cooled off that day. However, after a few days, the boyfriend was back in the apartment with her, as if nothing bad ever happened.

One afternoon, I knocked and knocked at Susan's door for about 5 minutes. The little girl opened the door and let me in. Even though it was about 2 pm, Susan and her boyfriend were sleeping on 2 different couches. The odor from alcohol was overwhelming. The boyfriend woke up first and when he saw me, he woke Susan up. It took Susan a few minutes to get her thoughts in order and she asked me how I got in. I told her that the little girl let me in and that I wanted my rent money. Susan said that she might have it tomorrow, and that I should go now because she had to go to work!? As I was leaving the apartment I heard her telling her little girl never to let anybody into the apartment. A few words that I heard Susan and her boyfriend exchange, made me understand that the boyfriend didn't know that Susan owed any rent. Apparently he gave her some money for rent, but she spent it for alcohol instead.

Well, the classy pretenses were confirmed wrong. I had to spend two more months evicting Susan through housing court system procedure and I never received any more of the money that she promised.

Morals of this story:

Classy or not, money speaks. Never let anybody move in before they pay all the required money. This rule applies especially for the ones who act classy, but request you to wait for the money. Take all the money before they move in, no exceptions!

Don't go out of your way fixing extra features of the apartment just because the prospective tenant appears classy. Have that tenant prove himself first by paying a few monthly rents on time. Then consider spending extra money on the apartment to make this good tenant happy.

Natasha and Her Daughter Sonya

The story I am about to tell you could be considered a horror story, because it was very costly for me as a Landlord and I didn't do anything wrong.

A blonde hair lady in her mid-thirties applied for a two-bedroom apartment. She stated in her application that she would like to get a first-floor apartment. I told her that I only had a fourth-floor apartment in my 8-unit brick apartment building, and unfortunately that was the only thing I could offer to her. She took that apartment and moved in with her 11-year old daughter Sonya. She asked me to let her know if and when a vacancy opened for a first floor or a second floor apartment. I agreed.

Three months went by. Every time Natasha was paying rent she would ask me if there was a vacancy on a lower floor and I told her there was none. She always acted disappointed.

One day Natasha called and said that there was a water leak in her kitchen and her bathroom, which were next to each other. I sent my maintenance man, George, to check the problem and have it fixed. It sounded to me that it was a problem with one of the water pipes. George went and over saw that there was water on the kitchen floor; bathroom floor, and some even on the living room floor. He called me and told me the bad news. Since he could not see any pipe that was leaking, he figured that some of the water pipes hidden in the floor or wall were broken and had to be found. Problems like that are very tricky and take some experience and luck to get fixed quickly.

George told me that the problem could not be easily solved. The floor in the kitchen would have to be opened up, and he suggested he started there. I told him to go ahead, because the problem had to be identified. After a couple of hours of ripping out the floor in the kitchen, trying to do as neat a job as he could, no water was visible. George told Natasha that he would have to get some extra tools and another helper and told her he would come back to continue the job. He also gave her his cell phone number instructing her to call him as soon as she notices some water coming again.

George went home to get some more tools and also called Juan, another helper I used occasionally. They met an hour later and just as they were getting ready to go to the building again, George received a call from Natasha. She was screaming into the phone: “The water is coming now. Come quick and see!”

George and Juan arrived about 20 minutes later. They saw water in the hole of the kitchen floor where George just made a hole, but there was also some water in the living room which could indicate that the water came somewhere through the wall. To make things even worse, there was some water visible on the floor of the bathroom too. That day was a cloudy day with occasional showers, so that both George and Juan started thinking that there could be both a leaky roof problem in addition to a plumbing problem.

The decision was made to make some neat holes in the living room and bathroom too, so that the destruction of the floors could be stopped as soon the leak was found. They worked about 2 hours enlarging holes in the floor of the living room and kitchen and making a new hole in the floor of the bathroom next to the bathtub drain. Unfortunately, they didn’t find any visible source of a water leak. George made a decision to stop at that time, instructed Natasha to be careful walking around those holes and to call them again when she noticed any water coming again. George and Juan finally left the apartment about 5 pm, telling Natasha that they would come back the next day around 9 am to continue the work.

I was informed about the work they did and that this work still didn’t produce any results. I told George on the phone that I will have to come the next morning to check things out myself, since I will be paying for this disaster.

There were no calls for the rest of that day. The next day about 9 AM George and I went to the apartment. Natasha let us in and said that some water must have come again early that morning. We both looked and saw the water in the bathroom next to the tub, in the hole, which George made, and also on the floor too. Some water was visible on the kitchen floor and on the living room floor also. I was very upset. George advised me that the next thing to do would be to remove the shower walls of the tub and look for the leak there. I told him to try that, and if there were still no positive results, to call Mark, the professional plumber that I used on harder jobs. I had to leave for work.

A couple of hours later George called me at work and told me that he removed the entire shower wall and lifted the tub, but didn't find any leak. He also told me that he called Mark, the Plumber, who could not come to the job until the next day. George had instructed Natasha that she and her daughter would have to be without a tub till at least the next day, when he would came back with the plumber.

The next day, Mark came together with George. Water was visible in all the places again, like the day before. In addition, there was some water in the hallway in front of the front door of the apartment. The plumber said that in addition to a possible leaky pipe in the floor, there could be a leak coming from the roof drain. The building had a flat roof and there was some rain over night, so that this assumption also made sense.

Mark, the plumber, and George got into action. They ripped out some walls on the outside of the apartment where Mark thought the roof drainpipe might be hidden. Unfortunately, they didn't find any roof drainpipe or any other water pipe there. Next, under Mark's instruction, more of the floor was opened in the living room, kitchen and bathroom. The entire bathtub was lifted out of place and set on the side. No leaky pipe was found. Mark and George decided to take a break and left for lunch.

When they came back, the fresh water was again visible in the kitchen and bathroom holes in the floor, and on the floor itself. George carried in a big box with some additional tools and left it on the bathroom floor. He and Mark worked for another hour and, since there was no water coming, they decided to stop for a while and go to another job. George told Natasha that he could be reached on the cell phone, and that she should call him when she noticed any new water.

Mark and George left. Mark was an independent contractor, so he told George to call him again when, and if, the leak was located. As far as he was concerned, he was done for now, and he had to go work on other jobs. However, George didn't leave the building as Natasha thought. He decided to wait a while in a small office room in the basement of the building.

George only waited about half an hour, when the call from Natasha came on his cell phone. "Water is coming, water is coming, come see it!" she was yelling. George went up the stairs to the apartment. He arrived in 2 minutes. He went into the bathroom and saw the fresh water in the bathroom and kitchen again. He just grabbed his toolbox from the bathroom and told Natasha that he would come back later. Natasha seemed upset that he was not going to stay and continue looking for the problem.

George went down to the basement office and plugged in the video camcorder that he had hidden in the toolbox. He apparently positioned the toolbox with the camcorder so that it could record the kitchen and bathroom floor. When he run the tape of the camcorder, he saw Natasha's and Sonya's feet moving around the bathroom with a bucket of water. Natasha was pouring water over the kitchen and bathroom floor and directing her daughter Sonya to spread the water around with her hands. Sonya's hands and face were visible at times, and voice directions from her mother were loud and clear. George went back to Natasha's apartment, re-mounted the tub and connected it, put some plywood over the holes in the bathroom, kitchen and living room, picked up all his tools and left. He told Natasha that he was not returning until after he talked to the landlord.

George and I watched the tape of the camcorder that day. We also made a regular VHS tape, so that it could be viewed from any VCR video player. Natasha called the next morning to talk to me. She asked about when we would be coming back to continue the job. She demanded that we fix the leaks or give her another apartment, on a lower floor. I told her on the phone that we would not come back for a while now, but that I would come that night to talk to her.

That evening, George and I went to Natasha's apartment with the videotape. We showed her the tape on her VCR player. I told her that I will be starting a speedy eviction process with her immediately and demanded that she pay for the damages to the apartment in addition to the rent that was already due.

I started the eviction process the next day, but it took another 30 days just to have a court hearing. Natasha didn't pay the rent that month and the next month either. She didn't show up for the court hearing, so I won by default. As I was preparing to get the Sheriffs Office arrange the formal eviction, I found out that she had moved out one evening. Needless to say, Natasha didn't leave a forwarding address. Repairs to the destroyed floors, walls and renovation of the bathroom, together with paying Mark, George and Juan cost me approximately $10,000.

What is the moral of this story? What did it teach me and anybody else who reads this story? Tenants have a strange way of trying to accomplish their goals regarding apartment accommodations. Many times the Landlord has to assume that there is a problem with a tenant, because that tenant has a certain motive for being destructive. In this case, the tenant wanted to be moved to an apartment on a lower floor of the building. Since she didn't get that wish accomplished by asking, she decided to do it the destructive way, not caring about how much that would cost the Landlord. This was a very irresponsible and immoral tenant, but you can get them sometimes. Every landlord should be aware of this kind of tenant.

I have to repeat again, check and double-check the references of each tenant that applies for your apartment. Hopefully you will avoid getting into this kind of situation.

Lorry and her son Steve

An older woman who looked about 75 was frequently visiting one of my tenants in the 12-unit apartment building. A couple of times she mentioned to me how she would like to rent an apartment from me, a two-bedroom for herself and her 26 year old son, Steve. My tenant (her friend) told me in confidence that Lorry would be a good tenant who would pay the rent on time and keep the apartment clean. Those are two most important virtues in a tenant. A few months later I had a two-bedroom apartment vacant and I sent a message to Lorry through my tenant, that I would like her to fill-out an application form.

The application form said that she was only 62 (strange, because she looked much older), and that both she and her 26-year-old son Steve were receiving monthly disability payments from the Federal Government. My tenant already had given her a good reference, so I didn't even bother checking other landlord references. Lorry and Steve moved in paying just the first month's rent, promising to pay the last month's rent in installments since times were hard. The rent was $465/month.

A few months passed and although I did receive monthly rents from Lorry about the fifth of each month, she never paid any money toward the last month's rent as she promised. She failed to sign a lease also. So here she was, after 3 months just a "Tenant at Will" with no money paid toward security deposit or last month's rent as initially promised. I had other problems to take care of, so I just let it ride. At least Lorry paid monthly rents and kept the apartment clean.

After 3 months Lorry told me that her gas stove was not working well. I promised to buy her a different, functional stove if she came up with the last month's rent which was way overdue. She told me that she would pay it, but she needed the stove quick. She also mentioned that it would be very unfortunate if she had to call a Board of Health inspector to check out the stove. This already sounded like a threat, so I bought another gas stove the following week. I didn't get any money toward the last month's rent again. However, trying to evict a tenant for not keeping promises, while paying monthly rents, would be difficult and against my business policy. Again, I let her ride; at least she was paying rent.

After 6 months Lorry gave me a rental check for $450 instead of $465. She told me that she could not afford $465. I argued a little, told her that this was not right, that she could not decrease the rent, but I took the check anyway. I was having trouble with some other tenants, who have not paid anything for a couple of months. I also needed to fix some apartments in order to rent them again. Problem with Lorry had a low priority. I was not going to spend my time trying to get extra $15 from the "little old lady."

A few months passed by and the little old lady became more demanding. She told me that both her bathroom and kitchen needed a new linoleum floor. I told her that I would look into it, but I didn't get to it for about a month. The next month Lorry gave me only $100 for the rent, and told me that the apartment was not worth more anyway. A few days later I decided finally to put Lorry on my list of "troublesome tenants." I gave her a "30 days Notice to Quit" followed by the Housing Court Eviction Process. I realized that somebody was coaching Lorry about not having to pay the rent if there were some things wrong with the apartment. She did not pay any more rents from then on.

After the Court Hearing date was set, I received a letter from the Building Inspector listing a lot of things wrong with Lorry's apartment. It listed that both the bathroom and kitchen had cracked linoleum floors and that ***the smoke detector was missing*** **.**

This was alarming, since every apartment is supposed to have a smoke detector. As soon as I read the letter from the inspector, I went to the store, bought a smoke detector and went to Lorry's apartment. I had the letter with me, looked at the bathroom and kitchen floors and looked up at the ceiling of the living room. The smoke detector was there, in plain view, where it always was. I asked Steve why the letter said that the smoke detector was missing. Steve just shrugged his shoulders and said that he didn't know. I realized that Steve must have removed the smoke detector before the inspector came, but put it back after the inspector left. Steve was apparently concerned about his safety, so he put it back again. I didn't know whether to be angry or to just laugh. I walked out, contacted my maintenance man George, told him what had happened and we both laughed. I arranged for George to fix the bathroom and kitchen floors a few days later.

The hearing date at the Housing Court finally arrived and I was in for another surprise. Lorry had a lawyer from Legal Services representing her, for free. In addition, there were representatives from the Department of Senior Services and from the Department of Mental Retardation, both there for the purpose of helping Lorry (a senior with a minor mental handicap) and her son Steve (with a minor mental handicap). However, the lawyer and both representatives acted very nice with me and told me that they were there, not only to help Lorry, but also to resolve the problem to everybody's satisfaction.

I had to present my case first, which I did. These tenants owed me about $1400 in back rents. Lorry's lawyer said that they were willing to pay the back rents if I agreed to keep them as my tenants. In addition, he said that the apartment, although clean and adequate, had some deficiencies that needed fixing. This was a very mild way of putting a tenants request for repairs so I felt good about it. The representatives from the Department of Mental Retardation and the Department of Senior Services both promised that they would help Lorry with some monetary support, and instructions on money management to pay all the back rents.

The judge ordered the Court Inspector to inspect the work done in Lorry's apartment. I went with him during the inspection. The inspector found that the work on both the kitchen and bathroom floors were acceptable except for a huge ugly wooden threshold between the bathroom and kitchen, which could trip people. I asked Steve where the other threshold was which was smaller and I knew had been recently installed. Steve shrugged his shoulders, and said again "I don't know." When we walked outside, the inspector instructed me that I should fix that threshold and everything would be fine.

As the inspector left, I went back to the apartment because I forgot the flashlight. Steve let me in because I told him that I was just coming back for my flashlight. Imagine my amazement when I saw the thinner, nicer threshold back in place between the bathroom and the kitchen. It was the threshold that George had installed the day before. Apparently, Steve figured that since the inspector was gone, there was no point in having to be tripping over the ugly thick threshold so he reinstalled the nice one. I just smiled and said to Steve: "I see you found the good threshold! Good job!" It is important not to have confrontations with the tenant if you don't have to.

Steve smiled back and said: "Yes I found it. It's OK now."

At the next hearing date at the Housing Court the Judge was presented with all the facts, that all the apartment deficiencies had been fixed and that Lorry had to pay about $1400 in back rent in addition to the current month's rent. I was a bit skeptical, and did not believe that they could pay all the back rents in addition to new rents that were coming due every month. We had scheduled meetings at the court every two months for the purpose of reviewing the progress of payments. To my surprise, Lorry managed to pay all the back rents over a period of 12 months in addition to her regular monthly rents. I decided to overlook the fact that her rent was still $450 instead of $465. A landlord should be practical and not get carried by emotions. The way I looked at this case was:

- If I had persisted in my intension to throw Lorry out at any cost, I would have never recovered the $1400 she already owed in back rents.

- If she never paid any more rent, by the time I had the court paper with the right to throw her out, another month and another $450 would be gone.

- Then, I would have had to pay the Sheriff's Office to formally throw her out (probably another $500).

- Then I would have to repaint the apartment (approximately $400 for painting) and advertise it for at least another month (another $450 in missed rent).

Anybody could see that letting her stay in the apartment was a good business decision. I also had more important things to do than to try to force Lorry to pay me $15 more for the apartment.

There are several morals to this story:

- You can't allow tenants to get on the "pay as much as I can and when I can schedule." You have to act forcefully when you notice that happening.

- You have to overlook minor things about the tenant's actions if the tenant is paying rents and catching up with back rents.

- You can expect the tenant to act with malice toward the apartment when the eviction process starts. You have to notice it and act upon it right away. In this case, the tenant's malicious actions were minimal. But keep in mind, they could be worse. See the story of "Natasha and her Daughter Sonya."

CHAPTER 9

The Commercial Mortgage Story As it Happened

In Chapter 3 I talked about a Commercial Mortgage. I described how different it is from a regular House Mortgage. I explained the dangerous clause that banks or commercial lenders include in the paperwork at the inception of the Commercial Mortgage. If you remember, the lender usually makes you sign papers that everything you own now and in the future is tied to this deal. In case you fall into financial hardship and cannot pay the monthly payments, you stand to lose everything you own with this kind of Mortgage. But the paradox is that, even if you send your monthly payments regularly for several years, the Lender has a review after 3 to 5 years at which time he has the right to call in the entire loan, due to poor market conditions (prices of Real Estate being down).

I learned this the hard way. I experienced having this kind of loan, which threatened to bring me to a financial ruin. When the economy slowed down and the entire country fell into a hard financial period, all the Real Estate values declined and many large and small investors lost everything. At that time I managed to formulate a course of action that allowed me to avoid financial disaster. I prepared and followed a complex financial plan that helped me to get through these rough times and emerge as a financial winner. I got rid of the Commercial Loan and kept all my Real Estate holdings, free and clear. I only had to keep a mortgage on my house.

How did I do it? Yes, that is exactly what I am going to tell you in this Chapter. I am going to show you how I did it. This story is true and you will benefit from seeing how it happened. It will give you some ideas on how to deal with situations like this. Enjoy the story. May be you can do something similar, for your financial benefit in your future Real Estate ventures.

Purchasing the Apartment Building

The story started in a year when the Real Estate market was booming. Housing and Commercial Real Estate was rising every month. It seemed that if I didn't get into the Real Estate market soon, I would miss a great opportunity.

I had a single-family colonial house in the city in which I worked in. My wife and I both had jobs with a salary. In a town near by I found an apartment building which was for sale. I liked the building and the surrounding area, but I felt that the asking price was a little high. The building had 8 one-bedroom apartments and three stores. It consisted of a 3-story brick structure that had 2 stores at the street level, 4 apartments on the second and third level and a separate one-story building next to it. The one story structure was rented by a small repair shop. The entire building was for sale at $360,000.

I took my time calculating the cash flow of the building and what a reasonable price would be. I finally decided to make an offer on the property and I called the listing real estate agent. The agent told me that the property was already under a Purchase and Sale Contract. The seller had accepted an offer of $360,000. The buyer had applied to a Lender for financing and the date for the closing was set.

I was upset, because the property was in a relatively good neighborhood. After 2 months, I almost had forgotten about it, when I heard again from the seller's agent that the deal hadn't gone through and that I could make an offer if I wanted to.

First I made an offer of $275,000, and it was rejected. After 2 weeks I made an offer of $300,000 and waited a whole week, no answer. Then I made an offer of $303,000 and wrote a personal letter to the seller explaining as well as I could, what a good offer it was. My offer was finally accepted subject to a substantial down payment to bind the offer (about $10,000). I refinanced my existing house for more money, came up with $60,000 cash for the down payment and obtained a commercial loan from a bank for $243,000.

At the closing the bank's lawyer gave us an unbelievable amount of paper work to sign. Our lawyer was trying to explain each paper as it came for signature. He was an older man, a guy in his seventies. His name was Tom. He was getting tired as more and more papers were presented to my wife and I to sign.

Tom reminded me of the older priest in the original movie "The Exorcist." Remember what happened to him? He got so tired trying to do his job that he had a heart attack and died. I didn't want anything bad to happen to my good old lawyer. Reading all those papers, listening to my lawyers explanations and signing the papers was wearing me out in addition to wearing out my wife out our poor old lawyer Tom. Well, at one point I decided to stop asking questions and signed all the papers. My wife reluctantly did so too, and Tom smiled because he was relieved. Well, at the end, I thought that I did get a good deal, because the property almost got sold for $60,000 more just a few months ago. I thought that was an indication of the good deal I was getting and nothing bad could happen with all these papers. Right?

Wrong! Oh, was I wrong!

The Real Estate market was on its way down, and I was not able to recognize that.

The bank made us sign papers that said that we were putting down not only the building as collateral, but also all our assets, personal home and our present and future earnings as a guarantee that we would repay this loan. Also, the papers said that if we didn't repay the loan before we died, our children would be obligated to repay it. In addition, this loan was up for a review every 5 years, even though it was set-up as a 20-year mortgage.

The 5 Year Review Process and how I handled it

At the time we bought the building my wife was pregnant with our third child. Almost immediately after the closing she took an 18 months leave of absence from her teaching job. It became really tough to handle the building and finances since I was a newcomer to this business. I had a $2600/month mortgage on the building + $550/month mortgage on the house. Fortunately, I had found a high paying job with a Utility Company and my wife went back to work the following year, so we were able to handle the building, using it mostly as a tax deduction. So, what does this say about a "lucrative real estate business?" It only means that if we didn't have reliable outside source of income during the first 3 years of operation, we would have probably lost the building during that time.

Those were the times when "the bubble had burst" in the Real Estate business. Thousands and thousands of private real estate investors and larger commercial real estate investors went into bankruptcy and foreclosures, lost their overpaid investments, lost their houses and similar. That was the time when someone who had money could have purchased an investment property very cheaply. But, not many people had money at that time, and those who did have it were investing in the stock market instead of Real Estate, since the Stock Market was on the rise.

In summary, the Real Estate market was heading downwards steadily. I kept paying both mortgages and kept in touch with my commercial loan officer. After 3 years he had the right to renegotiate my loan. This 3-year review went very well for me. My loan officer just gave me a slightly lower interest rate and informed me that my building was worth approximately only about 50% of what we had paid for it. No big fuss about it! The big 5-year review was coming soon and I didn't know the significance of it.

During that period of time we "sold" our house in the neighborhood that was becoming crime ridden, and we bought three-bedroom house in a nice neighborhood. We needed 4 bedrooms, but I figured that we could add two more bedrooms on to the existing house. The reason I put "sold" in parentheses, is because I was a victim of a so-called "professional tenant," a person who didn't put down any money to pay for the house, just a promise to buy, with a provision to move in and rent it for a year. This is another story which you have already read under the heading "Reverend Hardy." This house didn't have a high mortgage but was still a burden for a while, because the "professional tenant" was not paying any rent.

When the 5-year review was about 3 months away, I became very upset with the fact that practically 50% worth of my real estate investment had gone down the drain. I decided to write the bank a letter, explaining my hardship. I heard on the TV and also read in various books about instances where people got rich buying properties with no money down. I figured I could at least try to negotiate with the bank to decrease my commercial mortgage. I did very well with my commercial loan officer at the 3-year review! I was thinking, since I never missed a payment and both my wife and I had good jobs and good credit the bank would be willing to give us a break since the Real Estate market had gone down so much.

I wrote a letter to my loan officer asking the bank to renegotiate the loan with me in view of all these extraneous circumstances. The letter went out approximately 3 months before my 5-year review was due. That was another big mistake on my part. I should have kept quiet. This is what happened.

My regular loan officer (to whom the letter was originally sent) passed this letter and the whole case to a different department. Then, the bank sent what turned out to be practically "execution officers," 2 guys who initially reminded me of Joe Friday and Bill Gagnon in the show "Dragnet." All they wanted was the facts.

They gave me a bunch of papers to fill out, listing all my assets and income. They also arranged that the building be appraised, and the appraisal came to $127,000. As I got to know them further, when I talked about them I started referring to them as 2 henchmen.

The two henchmen collected all the facts: the outstanding loan was $207,0000 and the main collateral for it, the apartment building, was only worth 127,000. So their whole mission became obvious: they wanted to get as much money from me as possible, $60,000 to $80,000 cash. They requested that I re-finance my older house that was still not sold and my regular house that I was living in.

They said, with a smile, as if they were willing to do me a big favor: "Re-finance both houses; you can get at least $80,000 extra cash. Give us that cash and we will re-mortgage the building for the rest of the money ($207,000- $80,000= $127,000) for the remainder of 15 years. Believe us, this is an excellent deal, since nobody would put up a mortgage for the building for its value at this time. Any bank would request an additional 20% of the buildings worth as a down payment. Just do what we tell you and you have nothing to worry about!"

I remained calm in front of them, told them that I would have to consult with my wife and my accountant, and would get back to them within 2 weeks.

I knew that I didn't need an accountant or my wife to tell me one-way or the other. I knew that if I did what they asked me to do, I would be getting into deeper trouble, because the Real Estate Market was still heading down. The bank would get an even stronger grip on all of my holdings, 2 houses + apartment building. And if some tenants refused to pay rent because I had no money to fix the maintenance problems, I could lose everything in a few years. Besides, the "henchmen" were already talking about a full review in 3 years, which meant, if I held on for that long, they were going to ask for more money down at that time.

I talked to my wife, and she said that maybe we should do what they suggested because there was no other choice. My mother was living with us at that time. She was an old- fashioned woman, and she advised me to do what the bank requested, because banks always get what they want. I realized I had to make a decision on my own.

I went and talked to a commercial loan officer, David, a person I had befriended, who had nothing to do with my loan or the bank in question. I told him about what was happening to me, and about not having a good feeling regarding the "deal" the two bank henchmen were offering. David said that I was right. I should try to avoid that deal if possible, but he could not tell me whether I had any choice at that time. However, David gave me one piece of good advice. He said that I should go and talk to a lawyer, who specialized in bankruptcy. He went even further and told me to talk to a lawyer, who is the most hated by the bankers in the area. He gave me a list of 3 lawyers, with the most hated one on the top of the list. His name was Szatarra.

Next day I called the Law Offices of Szatarra and made an hour long appointment with Mr. Szatarra. Szatarra examined the facts briefly, told me that I had too much equity in my holdings at the time, and that I should try to improve my position in the next 2 to 3 years, if and when I ever got over the present problem. His advice was very valuable for the future, but at the present time, I was on my own, to do what I could.

Incidentally, in the same period that this was happening, I had applied for a city advertised grant for "Building Façade Improvements" and received a $30,000 Grant. The point of that grant, however, was that I had to spend 50% of my own money or $15,000 for window replacement (windows were old and drafty), brick pointing and general beautification of the building. That money had to be spent soon since it would make improvements to my building for 50% of my cost.

I examined the other facts. The building had no central heat. The installation of the central heating system had to be planned for the future at an estimated cost of $50,000. The electrical system also needed upgrading for an estimated cost of $ 8000. All those things needed money, and if I was to keep operating the building, a wise thing to do was to spend the money to perform all these improvements. On the other hand, the henchmen were requesting a large amount of money "for nothing." All they wanted the money for was to improve the loan to value ratio in their books, and to look good in front of their boss. They didn't care about me and my finances. Considering all these facts, I made up my mind that I had to act tough with the henchmen by all means.

I arranged a meeting with them. As I met with the two smiley "henchmen," I opened the discussion also with a smile on my face. "Gentlemen," I said, "I appreciate the deal you have offered me. However, my wife is very upset that we would have to increase the debt on the house we live in, because that means going deeper into trouble. Therefore, I am not willing to re-finance the house that I live in. Instead, I am willing to let you re-possess the building. I would give you the building without fighting and save you foreclosure expenses."

I was surprised at myself, that I said that so boldly. The thought of giving away my 5-year investment was not really appealing to me, but that idea came to me since Szatarra told me that the bank would not want my building. The bank wanted my home or my other house, not the problematic apartment building that they had mortgaged.

Surprisingly, the henchmen almost immediately changed their tune.

They said: "Well, we want you then to re-finance the other house which has about $30,000 extra equity. If you give us the $30,000, we will refinance the rest of your commercial debt for 10 years."

This was already a small victory for me. The bank was willing to forget about asking for $80,000 cash. They were willing to take just $30,000 which I could easily get from my other house, that had not been sold yet. All my worries could be over. But now, I wanted to try for more.

"Gentlemen, I can't really give you $30,000 because I have intended to improve the building that you are financing with a "City Restoration Grant" which requires that I put down $15,000 of the $30,000."

Henchman number 1 said hastily: " Then, you could give us $15,000?"

"Gentlemen, please," I continued, "the electrical system needs upgrading and the building also needs a central heating system. If I am to keep the building in operation in the present market, I have to plan investing another 40 to $50,000 into the central heating system in the next 3 years, in addition to $15,000 for windows and brickwork right now. It would be a great help if you would just re-mortgage my present debt. I would be paying you regularly every month, as I have done for the past five years. In 3 to 5 years from now, when you schedule another review, the building will be worth more anyway with all the improvements. Could you be reasonable and just re-mortgage the present debt, please?"

Henchmen number 2 said reluctantly: "Could you supply us with the paper work regarding that City Restoration Grant?"

"Certainly" I said with a smile, "I will find the paperwork as soon as I go home today, make a copy and send it to you."

It appeared that both henchmen had run out of ideas on what to say next. They realized that my position was firm. I was not ready to give them any money. What else was going through their minds, I could only speculate. They must have realized that having to take over the building and operate it while trying to sell it in the present shaky market, would be even more trouble for the bank. Also, their jobs would be much easier if they just re-mortgaged the loan and supported that decision with the paperwork which I was offering. Besides, in 3 to 5 years, who knows who would be handling a review of this particular loan! The bank was so large that either one or both of them could be promoted or changed to another department. Like in physics, everything goes by the path of least resistance! Since I was also a person with excellent credit, who had never missed a payment, I was not such a great risk to default in the foreseeable future. Everything was pointing in the direction that my request was reasonable.

The two henchmen stood up, shook hands with me and said: “Send us that paperwork! We will present this to our home office and let you know what the decision is in a couple of weeks.” They didn’t have smiles on their faces this time, but I decided not to worry about that.

I told my wife and my mother about how the meeting went, how I got the bank’s henchmen to lower their request from $80,000 to 15,000, and how I had refused. Both, my wife and my mother advised me to call the henchmen back and tell them that I will give them $15,000 from the equity in the other house. However, I decided to just send the paperwork as I had promised and to wait for their decision. So I did.

Two weeks later I was informed that the original debt was refinanced and that the next review of the loan was in 2 years! My wife and I were so happy. However, the 2-year review was now a serious matter to think about in addition to all the other renovations and the selling of our old house. I decided to make a plan following recommendations from Szatarra. I was going to fully prepare myself for the next review.

Making Up a Plan for the next Bank Review

I didn't want to wait for 2 years to be in a similar or worse position than I was now. I gathered in my mind all the things that the lawyer Szatarra told me, and all the things that David, a friend who was a commercial bank loan officer of another bank, told me. I prepared a plan that I thought would help me outsmart the bank and save myself from financial disaster.

I wrote down things that I had to do. Outsmarting the bank and bank officers who I called "henchmen" was a necessary thing. I looked at it as: "It is a battle and either the Bank or I will prevail." If the Bank were to prevail, they wouldn't feel bad about me, the little guy, who would lose all his belongings. I would just become a statistics in some government's survey on how many people went bankrupt due to the poor economy.

I got into positive thinking. I began to think that I would prevail and make it better for myself. The Bank will come out as a loser and lose their investment, the Commercial Mortgage that they gave me. I had always paid all my bills up to that moment and paid them on time. However, this time I would have to change that because it was a matter of my financial survival. I was thinking that it was better that the Bank get hurt rather than my family and me. I had taken a risk 7 years ago when I purchased the building, and the Bank took a risk too. It was not right for me to be the one to get hurt.

With such positive thinking, I made and followed the plan which is explained on the following pages.

Step One, Selling the old House

The first order of business was to sell the other house and make sure the excess money from the sale was either invested or spent, or somehow not visible! Yes, I did manage to make over $30,000 on the difference between the sale of that house and the mortgage I owed. Some of that money went into "façade restoration" of the apartment building, but some of the money went into my pocket.

Step two, Talking to my Business Partner

The next order of business was to talk seriously with my wife and make her agree on the course of action I was to choose. My wife never wanted to have anything to do with the investment property. However, since we owned our house jointly and we both had signed on the Commercial Mortgage, she was essentially my "Business Partner" whether she wanted it or not.

I sat down with her and said: "Honey, we need to refinance our house, and take out in cash all the money that the bank will give us."

At that moment we owed only about $69,000 on the house, which was worth about $130,000. I told her that the bank would probably give us about a $100,000 mortgage for 30 years. I also told her that, in addition, I wanted to get a home equity or a second mortgage in the maximum amount, may be another 15 to 20 thousand dollars.

My wife was stunned. She said: "But I was hoping that we would have the house paid-off in about 10 years from our 15-year mortgage. You are going in the opposite direction with this. This is crazy. What are we going to do with all the money? We will have money coming out the ka-zoo. We are talking about $50,000 or more, all in cash. What do we do with all the cash?"

I said, "To put your mind at ease, first off I will give you 50% of all the cash we end up with, so you can deal with it as you wish. From my half, we will add some bedrooms to our existing house and we will take vacations!"

Now everybody should realize how important it is to have a partner in business whom you can trust. If you have a partner in your financial ventures, two of you have to agree on a lot of things and you have to trust each other. A lot of partnerships get broken at the first serious trouble. Then, either one partner cheats the other and the cheated one gets financially ruined and sues the other, or the partnership just falls apart and everybody loses. If you are alone in your ventures, you make all the decisions. In my case, even though my wife didn't want to be a part of my Real Estate venture, she was a part of it indirectly because the house we lived in was jointly owned. Therefore, it was important at that moment that she agree to follow my plan.

My wife liked the idea of a house addition and vacations. However she still asked; "Why are you doing it? Are you sure this is the right thing to do?"

I replied: "I want to do this so that in 2 years the bank henchmen can not take the house we live in, no matter what happens with the apartment building!"

She finally agreed to go along with me, although still thinking and saying that I was totally crazy for doing what I was doing.

Step 3, Re-Financing, Charging, Spending

During the next year I refinanced our house for 30 years and took a home equity line of credit, which I maxed out. I renovated our house adding 2 bedrooms, an in-ground swimming pool, a large sunroom and a detached garage. I also took my wife and 3 children to Disneyland in Florida and to the Bahamas for the New Years Eve, charging these expenses on credit cards. You can imagine how puzzled all of our friends, neighbors and relatives were. They could not understand how could we be spending so much money. We were really "living it up."

I must underline that no matter how this excessive spending of money appeared on the surface, it was still very much under control. My wife got half of the money and was probably using some and stashing some away for "dark days to come." I was spending a lot (that's how it looked) but I also had some money hidden away so that nobody would know about it. The charges on credit cards that climbed to about $5000 to $10,000 I always transferred to cards that had minimal (promotional) rates of interest which was 0% to 6% a year for 6 months.

Step 4, Stop Paying the Commercial Mortgage

After about a year when I was satisfied with the amount of financing and credit in which we were indebted, I stopped paying the commercial mortgage, which was about $2200 a month. I kept paying our home mortgage of about $900/month including home taxes. You could imagine what it felt like to all of a sudden have $2200 extra every month. I stopped paying $2200 in December of that year and didn't even hear from any bank officer until April of the following year.

Regular monthly bills kept coming in the mail. The bank was diligently sending monthly mortgage bills and warning me of additional penalties and interest charges that were accumulating. In April of that year a bank officer left a message on my answering service. He was asking me to call him back and settle what he called "an omission" on my part. I made sure to call that number during lunch time, when nobody was in the office. I left a message that I called back, that I was in a little financial bind but would take care of the problem by the next month. I realized already that the person calling me was neither one of the two henchmen from just a year ago. This was a completely new voice, apparently from a bank officer who had just received this account.

Believe me, I didn't receive another phone call until September, which was already 10 months after I stopped paying the mortgage. I realized later what was happening. My loan of $220,000 + all penalties and interest didn't have such a high priority. Many accounts that this bank had to handle were in the million dollar figures, so my account was still waiting for its turn. This was fine with me, since every month meant another $2200 extra in my pocket.

Step 5, Cooperating with the Bank – my way

The phone call and the letter I received in September did sound serious. The letter said that if they didn't hear from me or get some kind of cooperation within the next 10 days that they were going to start foreclosure proceedings. I decided to take the next step in my plan: "Start cooperating with the bank!"

I was planning to cooperate, but in my own special way. I planned to give the bank every cooperation possible in respect to meeting with bank officers and adjustors, showing them the building and showing them printouts of my bank account statement. Only one minor thing I was not going to do: I was not going to pay them any money toward the mortgage and penalties that I owed. Here are some anecdotes of those dealings with the bank, which tended to show my cooperation.

The bank officer, Sam, finally reached me on the phone that September and the conversation went like this:

Sam: "Sir, I understand you are having difficulties with finances. You understand you owe us. Could you tell me what you intend to do?' This question was right to the point, there was no "beating around the bush."

Me: "I don't think I can pay you, but I am at least willing to try to resolve this some other way if possible."

Sam: "Do you think you can sell the building for us and give us the money?"

Me: "Maybe I could sell it, but you won't be able to get very much money from that sale."

Sam: "How about your house, how much is it worth?"

Me: " It is worth about $140,000"

Sam: "How much do you owe on it?"

Me: "I have a first mortgage of about $105,000 and a second mortgage of about $15,000."

Sam: "Would you be willing to let us appraise your building and your home and run a credit check on you and your wife?"

Me: "Yes, certainly. I will cooperate in every way possible. I am willing to give you the building and save you foreclosure costs if you give me something else in return."

Sam: "What do you expect in return? You owe us over $240,000?"

Me: "I was hoping that if I give you the building back without any hassle, you would wipe out my debt to you completely!"

Sam: "It does not work quite that way, Sir. However, I am very glad you are able to speak with me in such a calm way. I have had a lot of clients who got so excited when talking to me that they totally lost it!"

Me: "Lost what? What happened to them?"

Sam; "One of my clients had a mental breakdown and had to seek psychiatric help. The other one did worse than that!"

Me: "What do you mean worse? How could it be worse?"

Sam: "He had a heart attack and subsequently died. We had to deal with his widow! "

Me: "Well, I will try to keep calm until we resolve this. I hope I won't have to go into foreclosure and bankruptcy, because in that case I don't think you would get much when you take over the building."

Sam: "I know that, Sir. I also know that the building is now operating; you are collecting some rents. So, will you cooperate with us, show the building to our appraiser, show us your rent rolls, and also other personal things regarding your home and your finances?"

Me: "I already said I would do all that. Also, if you don't want to take over the building, I will help you sell it."

Sam: "Again, I want to thank you Sir for your cooperation and your calmness. I will have the appraiser contact you shortly."

That conversation went well. I found out how much the bank officer appreciated cooperation in any way. If I didn't cooperate in this way, and some people don't, the bank would have to go through foreclosure, take the building back temporarily and put it up for sale at a Public Auction. However, once the bank has to take that route, the owner would usually take every dollar he could from the remaining tenants. He would not spend any money on any maintenance or repairs during that period. So, by the time the bank would take over the building maybe in 3 to 6 months, the property would end up in very poor shape. Most of the tenants would be gone by that time or would be litigating in the Housing Court. Bankers know this process very well. Sam apparently knew it too, and I realized that by cooperating with him now would benefit me in the end. I figured that I should be able to negotiate some favorable terms for later.

During the following two weeks I met with the bank appraisers. I showed them all the bad things about the building (possible leaky roof, inadequate heating system, some vacancies and non-paying tenants). I didn't mention any good things about the building. I left it for the appraiser to evaluate and notice the good things on his own. Anyway, the building got appraised at $90,000. The Real Estate market was at the lowest. Very few buildings were getting sold, and many foreclosures were happening at that time. Still, it was really sad to think how the property that I bought for $303,000 only six years ago, could buy now be bought for $90,000 or even less. The thought of this made me sick!

Sam, the bank officer, also arranged for our credit to be checked. He found out about all our outstanding debts and how we were paying on them. The fact was that, although we had a lot of debt, we were on time and up to date with all other loans. We were not delinquent on any other payments except this big one, the commercial mortgage. You would not believe, but Sam felt good about my credit report, even though I owed almost $240,000 on his loan and I was not making any payments.

It was already late October when I had another important conversation with Sam. It went like this:

Sam: "Sir, since we have all the facts now, we would like to resolve this promptly so that it is on our books this calendar year. Could you sell the building?"

I felt there was a possibility here, so I lied: "Yes, I have an investor who is offering me some money, but it is a pretty low offer!"

Sam: "How much is he offering?"

Me: "$40,000."

Sam: "Is that buyer credible, can he come up with CASH?"

Me (Lying even further): "Yes, he can come up with CASH."

Sam: "Sir, we are willing to give you an opportunity now to get rid of your debt to us. If you could sell the building for $40,000 and come up with $20,000 from your own sources, for a total of

$60,000 we will write–off your loan. The only thing is, you have to get everything done by December 31 of this year!"

Me: "Sam, thank you very much for this opportunity. Let me talk this over with my potential buyer and with my wife. The $20,000 to come out of our pockets at this time might still be impossible. I will let you know!"

Getting Rid of Debt – the Final Accomplishment

I told my wife about Sam's final offer. My wife was agreeable. She said that $20,000 was a miniscule amount to pay to get rid of the building and get rid of the $240,000+ debt that the building carried with it. But I wanted more. I figured I was in the driver's seat again.

I negotiated with Sam a few days later, tried to get him to take only $10,000 of my own money. I talked in a sad voice, how the times were very hard, and here I was about to lose the biggest investment of my life and still pay for it. Sam reluctantly went down to a figure of $16,000, but said that was final. I had to sell the building for $40,000, pay another $16,000 from my own pocket and get it all done by the end of the year.

Now, the biggest task remaining was to find a buyer, who had at least $40,000 or could come up with it quickly. I wanted to keep the building too, if I could, but that was against Szatarra's recommendation. He told me at that meeting 2 years prior that under no circumstances could I be a buyer of my own building. He told me that I should sell it, get rid of it and get rid of debt!

I still thought that there was a way. I had to find a buyer who could be talked into doing a favor for me. A favor so big that only a friend could do it. Not only that this buyer had to be a friend, he would also have to be a friend whom I could trust.

I asked around, friends who I knew had money. All those friends whom I had known for 10 to 20 years refused to buy the building from me, claiming either that they had no money or that this business was too risky. Relatives of my wife were also out of the question, because none of them had any money. My relatives were back in Europe, and they had no money either. It was not easy. It was already November. I had not come up with a friend-buyer and it looked like I would just have to sell the building to anybody and lose my life investment.

In the last moment, I thought of a friend who lived 1000 miles away. His name was Bob. I called him. I explained to him the scenario that was supposed to happen. He was expected to buy the building from me for $40,000 and in a short period of time, about six months, sell it back to me. I told him that I would pay for all his expenses of coming to my town and doing this business. I also told him that when the time came that he could sell the building back to me, the price could be negotiated on the basis of what he wanted for a profit! He agreed, because he was a friend. He agreed, not because he saw an opportunity to make a quick profit. He agreed because he wanted to help me. He wanted to help a friend in financial trouble.

I arranged everything for the sale of the building. I made up a Purchase and Sale agreement for $40,000 and sent it to Bob for his signature. I also hired Szatarra for my lawyer and I hired my old lawyer, Tom, for the buyer's lawyer. The selling process still had to take time and we managed to arrange a closing date for the 30-th of December. That left only one day, the last day of the year, for the lawyers to do all the other processing of paperwork required for the bank.

Bob came by plane on December 29-th and stayed in my house. He was about $14,000 short, but I told him that I would cover that. He handed $26,000 in cash to my wife and me that night. We put the money away for the closing, had dinner and went to sleep.

The next day we did some running around to collect all the cash that we needed. This time we did not even bother asking for any money from those friends that refused to help previously. My wife and I collected all the money from various places that we had it stashed away. Then we went to the bank.

In the bank we bought one cashier's check for $40,000 and one for $16,000. Bob wasn't worried about anything, he was sitting on the chair in the bank reading a newspaper, while my wife and I were frantically opening envelopes and giving the cash to the bank's teller. You should have seen that young teller's face as she was counting the cash we gave her. She probably never saw that much cash in her life all at once, even though she worked in the bank. We were opening envelopes full of $100 bills, handing it to the teller as if it were pocket change. She had to count all the money. She also got the bank's manager of that branch to check all the counted money and validity of the bills.

When we were done, we had lunch and then went to the closing.

Szatarra and Tom, our two lawyers were at the closing. The bank didn't even send any representative. It appears that Szatarra acted as the bank's representative. He told me that I had done my negotiations so well that any request that he had on the phone from the bank was immediately granted to him. This closing was a breeze for him. Still, the charge for his involvement was $2500, while Tom only charged $600. I had to pay for both lawyers, and they did accept my personal checks for that part.

Szatarra took all the papers. He told me that he would rush everything to the bank and that I could expect the bank release on the loan in about 10 days.

It all happened so fast; it looked like a dream.

“What do I do now?” I asked Szatarra as he was leaving.

“You don’t have to do anything; you are done; you are out!” Szatarra said with a smile and he left with all the papers.

He was right. As far as he was concerned and as he had advised me previously, I was now out of debt and out of business. However, I had my follow-up plan.

My wife and I took Bob to the insurance agency so we could arrange that the building’s insurance continue, with Bob as Owner and me as Manager. Then we took Bob to the airport so he could get back to his family for the New Year’s Eve party.

Bob said to me: “Now go ahead and run the building as before as if you were still the owner. In about 3 to 6 months I will come back and I can sell you ***your building*** back.”

This was fantastic, Bob was a friend who didn’t try to take advantage of me and take any money. And also the way he talked, calling the building “my building,” made me feel indebted to him greatly.

In about 10 days we received the papers from the bank releasing us from all the responsibility for the loan, in consideration of the $56,000 that they received from me. There was a so-called “forgiven debt” of about $190,000 that was associated with this deal, and we had to claim it on the taxes that year as income. However, as there was also a large loss associated with our sale (buying for $303,000 and selling for $40,000) our taxes turned up a considerable return that year.

The three months passed quickly. I talked to Bob and told him that I was ready to take the building back. I bought him another airplane ticket to come to my town so we could do it. Bob came, sold me the building for $40,000 + a small profit he wanted, that we agreed on. We did the transaction in cash using a Quit Claim

Deed. We didn’t use any lawyers. We registered the sale at the City Hall Registry of Deeds. Now I owned the building again, and this time without any mortgage. This completes my story on commercial mortgages, creative financing and debt elimination.

Concluding Thoughts on Commercial Mortgage and Debt Elimination

What does this story show you about mortgages and money? One can learn a lot about dealing with a bank, lawyers and "financial creativity." Getting rid of debt, acquiring investment properties with little or no money is possible, but within certain boundaries. One has to be careful and do a lot of planning, before one of these or similar plans can be worked out. One cannot just simply follow rules from a myriad of books, which tell you how to use OPM (other people's money), acquire properties with no money, sell those properties and put profits in your pockets. Most of the time these are just fairy tales.

Why did I succeed here? I will state the reasons:

- I happened to talk to a friend, a bank officer who recommended a lawyer that all the banks hated.

- I selected a good lawyer who was able to give me valuable guidelines to follow in order to avoid financial disaster.

- I took all the advice under consideration and made up a solid plan to deal with the bank.

- I followed that plan in every detail.

- I found a friend willing to help, who made my plan even more successful.

- I was at the right place at the right time.

CONCLUSION

There, you have it. I hope you enjoyed reading it. I also hope that this book teaches you about the reality of Real Estate Investing and makes you aware of stumbling blocks on your way to success. Good luck in investing. It can be both fun and profitable.

Author